the **armstrong & miller** book

the armstrong & miller book

Alexander Armstrong and Ben Miller

With additional material by Jeremy Dyson

sphere

First published in Great Britain in 2010 by Sphere

Copyright © Toff Media Limited, 2010

Written by Alexander Armstrong and Ben Miller
with additional material by Jeremy Dyson.

Material based on characters and sketches by:
Ben Miller and Alexander Armstrong;
Jeremy Dyson; David Cadji-Newby and Nico Tatarowicz;
Andy Riley and Kevin Cecil; Bert Tyler-Moore and George Jeffrey;
Simon Blackwell; David Scott and Ali Crockatt; Simeon Goulden;
Jamie Lennox and Louis Waymouth; Mark Bussell and Justin Sbresni;
Laurence Rickard and George Sawyer; Richard Pinto and Anil Gupta;
Graham Linehan; Carl Carter and Tony Cook; Jason Hazeley and
Joel Morris; Aidan Hawkes; Ben Edwards and Simon Ludders;
Gareth Gwynne; Alistair Griggs.

The moral right of the authors has been asserted.

A CIP catalogue record for this book is available from the British
Library, isn't it.

ISBN 978-1-84744-431-8

Sphere
An imprint of
Little, Brown Book Group
100 Victoria Embankment
London EC4Y 0DY

An Hachette UK Company
www.hachette.co.uk

www.littlebrown.co.uk

Cover photography
and frontispiece
Colin Thomas

Photography
Tim Barnes
Adam Lawrence
Rory Lindsay
Madeleine Waller

Stock images
© Nasjonalgalleriet, Oslo, Norway/© DACS/The Bridgeman Art Library p69
© Bettmann/Corbis p80
© CORBIS/SYGMA p116 top, p117 top
© Julian Smith/ea/Corbis p116 bottom
© Patrick Durand/Sygma/Corbis p117 bottom
Time Life Pictures/Getty Images p124, p339
Getty Images p165
© SSPL via Getty Images p207
Redferns/Getty Images p241
© Pushkin Museum, Moscow, Russia/The Bridgeman Art Library p244

Various images for 'Expedition to Amsterdam' provided under
a Creative Commons license by flickr.com contributors
Karen Horton, Terrazzo, 666isMONEY, Ryan Somma, rinuseversen1,
Rob Lee, Stuck In Customs, Heatheronhertravels
and Minke Wagenaar.

Photographic assistance
Beatrice Brierley, Julia Cook, Emma Dogliani, Chloe Franks, David Saxby
and Hackney Carpet Warehouse Ltd.

Illustration
Lydia Barnes 'Flint and Rory's Really Wild Cookout'
Flip CG @ Debutart Sportsfest mascot
Josh Knowles Unfunny cartoons and 'The Songs of Brabbins and Fyffe'
Anastasya Martynova Brady the Bear, Boudoir d'Amour and Sportsfest logos
Max Schindler 'Warmonger' comics
Katherine Tulloh 'Boudoir d'Amour', 'The Critical Factor', 'The Origins of ...' and 'The Joy of Sex'

Translation
Caroline Achaintre

Musical arrangement
Simon Wallace

Design
Tim Barnes, chicken ⚡ www.herechickychicky.com
for Katherine, Lydia, Christie and Barbary

Printed and bound
in Italy by Lego SpA

For

Professor Lord Robert Winston
Our favourite Professor Lord

xxx

B & X

'Shall we ... ?'

Thirsty ● Sated

QUENCH YOUR THIRST

💬 IM   📧 Email   👁 Views   ▼▼ Bites   ✦ Online

MEMBERS ONLINE   SEARCH   MY PROFILE   MY ACCOUNT

fitpharius23 - 2475 - Straight - Buckinghamshire

Relationship status	I'd rather not say ▼
Occupation	private income
Height	5'9" ▼
Body type	toned ▼
Hair colour	flax ▼
Eyes	magenta ▼
Personality	shy ▼
Entertainment	books / cooking / theatre / opera
Sport	none ▼
Smoking	never ▼
Special powers	gliding, shapeshifting

My statistics

Number of visits: **11**
Number of bites: **0**

More about me   MODIFY

What do you do for fun?
In my prime I was a duellist by rapier and dagger. Last week I attended a salsa class.

Favourite local hot spots or travel destinations?
**This much I know: the Danube is wonderful in the spring. The foothills of the Eiger can be restful in season.
A1 Bowling in Marlow is like hell on earth.**

Tell us more about your job
I have no 'job'. I have a vocation: the shepherding of souls into the yawning throat of Hades itself. I also have 80wpm typing.

SAVE

A few words about me   MODIFY

Your dating headline (2 to 128 characters)
Please release me from this hell.

Describe your character, talk about what you enjoy or explain what you're looking for ... This description will tell other members more about you (50 to 2000 characters)
I am the motherless child of a she-devil hauled from the very coals of the smouldering infant earth. I have walked the shifting dust of a desolate creation and seen kingdoms rise into empires, and empires razed to destruction. Looking for under 30s in the Beaconsfield area.

SAVE

About my date   MODIFY

Her age	25–30
Her weight	50–55 kg
Her relationship status	Single
She lives ...	Locally
Her body type	Slim
Her skin type	Fair
Her blood group	O
Should she be romantic?	Yes
Does she smoke?	No
Her diet	Healthy
Her hair style	Long

My lifestyle   MODIFY

My taste in music	Madrigals, old English plainsong
My favourite films	Birth Of A Nation
My perfect night out	Ballroom dancing
Diet	Virgin's blood
My pets	Owl
My exercise habits	Walking
Romance	Yes
Do I want children?	With the right bride
Religion	None
Income	18 testoons per annum

4

FEED Meet mortals who are histologically compatible with you! GO

Thirsty ● Sated

QUENCH YOUR THIRST

IM | Email | Views | Bites | Online

MEMBERS ONLINE | SEARCH | MY PROFILE | MY ACCOUNT

hunglikeahorschstadt - 872 - Curious - Dulwich, London

Relationship status	single
Occupation	self-employed
Height	5'11" (6'1" when gliding)
Body type	husky
Hair colour	badger
Eyes	onyx
Personality	outgoing
Entertainment	bars / clubbing / gardening / gigs
Sport	Hot Box Yoga, Pilates
Smoking	trying to give up
Special powers	I bake a mean banana bread

My statistics

Number of visits: **0**
Number of bites: **0**

More about me   MODIFY

What do you do for fun?
Flash-mob roller-blading, ten-pin bowling, salsa, capoeira. Is that still hip? I mean hep? Hip?

Favourite local hot spots or travel destinations?
In 1905 spent a wonderful summer in lupine form in the White Carpathian mountains, cavorting and foraging in the mote-laden dusk. Nearer to home, a friend and I have a deposit on a holiday cottage in Bude, Cornwall, for the second week of August.

Tell us more about your job
Fortune has granted me one task alone; the chaperoning of beautiful women to the gates of ecstasy. Furthermore I have access to a reliable babysitter and am a very good listener.

SAVE

About my date   MODIFY

His/her age	Any
His/her weight	Any
His/her relationship status	Any
He/she lives ...	Any
His/her body type	Any
His/her skin type	Any

A few words about me   MODIFY

Your dating headline (2 to 128 characters)
Old Skool till I die. Which I won't. Ever.

Describe your character, talk about what you enjoy or explain what you're looking for ... This description will tell other members more about you (50 to 2000 characters)
With-it hipster seeks contemporary chick for texting, F2F, Skype and partying/clubbing. Oh, and the sating of my blood-lust. But that bit's not important, really it's not. I'm just here for the vibe. I'm chilled. Truly.

SAVE

My lifestyle   MODIFY

My taste in music	Coldplay
My favourite films	When Harry Met Sally
My perfect night out	Floodlit cricket at Lord's
Diet	Blood
My pets	None
My exercise habits	Gym 3x week
Romance	Would be nice
Do I want children?	Not yet
Religion	Other
Income	£26,000 per annum basic
Piercings/tattoos	?
Turnoffs	?

5

Boys and girls with inquiring minds and a light touch will enjoy this fun and informative guide to the intriguing art of **origami**, or Japanese paper folding

Radio's **'Professor' Dennis Lincoln-Park**, well-loved for his appearances on *Why?*, coaches you expertly through a carefully graded series of enchanting paper models, and contributes a fascinating history of the craft.

•89P

Modern Mandala Press

Origami – anchor of "the floating world"

'Origami' (pronounced *or-i-gam-e* – not unlike the Italian herb) is a Japanese word which means paper-folding. The Japanese do not consider it an art-form but rather an integral part of their culture – like ritual suicide.

Associated in the first instance with the making of intricate paper dolls and folded tokens – or *noshis* – origami originated amongst prisoners condemned to death – as a means of passing the time until their demise in a reasonably pleasant manner (it is the Japanese custom that a condemned prisoner would not be informed of his death until the morning of the

execution – so he would wake each day not knowing if it was to be his last. A few hours folding diverting shapes with a square of paper six inches by six inches may have been just the thing to keep up the spirits in the brutal and unforgiving environment of death row). Since then origami has become an accepted pursuit for the young and an intellectual hobby for many adults – be they innocent or guilty of a capital charge.

Westerners do not easily follow diagrams so I have elected to have a series of photographs taken of myself demonstrating just how simple this

'The Embrace'

i

6

Origami Academy

Dennis Lincoln-Park

wonderful pastime is. In the pages that follow I hope to demonstrate how, from an elementary beginning many beautiful objects can be fashioned.

In order to most accurately describe how to fold these pieces I have been fortunate enough to be allowed to take these pictures in the Shunga Museum of Origami in Funabashi – a treasure trove of jewels and riches of this ancient art with many examples of pieces dating back to the eighth century BC.

Indeed you will see on the table to the left of my hands several such items folded by Emperor Kammu himself at the height of the Heian Period (AD 782–1185). On my right is an original edition of the *Kan No Mado* manuscript from the same period – handwritten on paper made from

shredded silk. If it is proven true – and I believe it can be – then what you are looking at are among the oldest existing examples of paper folding in the Oriental world. Naturally these items' value – and indeed their price – are absolutely beyond measure.

A WORD ON PROCEDURE

When you have mastered the basic folds you will be equipped to produce a lifetime of figures and shapes of your own. Watch out for terms like Squash Fold, Petal Folds and Rabbit's Ears and learn them well. Take it slowly; fold carefully, neatly and accurately, and *start at the beginning!* The longest journey commences with but a single step.

—DL-P, Fen Ditton

Japanese 'Sanbow'
(Offering Tray)

1.
Begin with the paper
coloured side down.
Make two creases diagonally
from corner to corner.

2.
With the corners folded into
the centre, turn the paper over
and fold corner to corner.

5.
Turn over once again. Fold
the opposing flaps together.
Fold the back flap forward
and toward the crease lines.
Reverse and repeat.

6.
Put all the corners together,
half open and lift out.

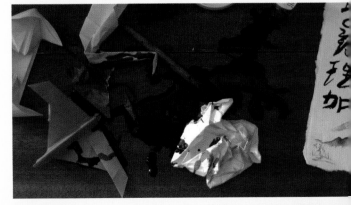

3.

Lift the top flap up and squash the point flat in on itself. Then turn the paper over once again and lift the revealed flap up.

4.

Squash point D flat (see figs. 6a and 7) and open out X and Y.

7.

Pull the top flaps down and, finally, repeat behind to form the central bowl.

The 'Sanbow'.

Market forces

Words Chrissie Duff-Moynihan
Photographs Simon Addams

What started as a farm-gate protest movement to bypass greedy retail margins has grown steadily into a pan-suburban weekend staple. Where would we be, just twelve years later, without our blessed legions of Farmers' Market men and women?

EGGS

wheat
Free
1.65 cakes

COFFEE OF PERU

ORGANIC

Fresh Bufacto
Mozzarella
"Bocconcini"
£3.50
FOR 5KW

TEA

Builder's ~
Earl Grey ~
Peppermint ~
Camomile ~ 1.
Rooibos ~ 1.0
Green ~ 1.00
grape

"This beats showing people round houses any day – and it's a helluva buzz sending people away with crap you've just thrown into a basket!"

Huw David, 42

Chocco-lotto artisanal patisserie

Huw reckons he knows all about chocolate. He should – he's been making the stuff for nearly two years.

'Never call me a chocolatier,' he says with an arch wink. 'It makes me sound like I should be poncing around in a billowing shirt!'

Huw's stall is considered the honey-trap of the marketplace; his fellow stall-holders jockey each week to be next to the towering piles of Huw's mouth-watering Chocco-lotto treats.

'Basically, I just make what people want,' laughs Huw as he sticks a naughty schoolboy finger into a chocolate rice-crispie cake. 'But quality never comes cheap,' he winks, again. 'I only ever use genuine Kellogg's Rice Krispies. Or sometimes Aldi at a pinch.'

He's got a point: six of these dinky ambrosial cakes, melting now and shining sensuously in the morning sun, will cost you £24. But somehow I dare you not to buy them …

ORGANIC EGGS
EX LARGE £2.20/BOX
LARGE £1.85/box
MEDIUMS £1.65/box
SMALLS £1.00/box

ORGANIC EGGS
£1 per Box

Banana Almond Cake

Almond Croissant

RAW VEG & TOASTED SEEDS

Thai Red Curry Pork Scotch Egg

PICKLES

Jeremy Peakes, 39
The Veritable Aladdin's Cave of Cheese

Jeremy grew up on the South Downs and still lives there with his wife Frieda. 'It's God's Own Country – no argument,' he affirms.

Jeremy's obsession with local produce even extends to the Peakes' family transport. Both he and his wife drive Nissans, 'which I'm pretty sure are built in this country. They certainly used to be!'

Jeremy and Frieda use their cars to travel to Calais where they buy 'industrial quantites' of cheese. 'Camemberts, Bries, Gorgonzolas ... all that sort of stuff, even La Vache Qui Rit,' he laughs.

Certainly his stall, The Veritable Aladdin's Cave of Cheese, is truly a treasure trove of cheese; they've got all kinds of cheese; it's a cheese-lover's dream, covering the full A–Z of cheeses. It's like stumbling across a secret – and entirely unexpected – cavern full of cheese. And then some!

Jeremy and Frieda have been selling cheese at the Farmers' Market for seven months.

> "People have had enough of buying The Stepford Vegetables – they want things that are a bit manky and covered in shit."

Milo Tippett, 44
Agriculturalia

'I've never considered myself a greengrocer,' explains former property sales manager Milo. I made the mistake of calling him an estate agent and was treated to a detailed job description. I think it's fair to say Milo knows his job market nearly as well as his Farmers' Market!

'I just sell what's in season, what's lying around.'
The week I visit the Farmers' Market he is selling some beautiful organic woollen finger puppets, a snip at £6 each or five for £29.50.

Kevin Gatenby, 35
Owner of Wine & Cards newsagents and convenience store

'I'll be honest with you,' says Kevin, looking over his shoulder (I'm beginning to feel like I'm stuck in an unusually fruity Albert Square storyline). 'When the Farmers' Market started up a couple of years ago I was dead against it.' With other local tradesmen Kevin even started a petition to ban it. Unsuccessfully as it turns out.

'But it's been a blessing.' Market Day is now his busiest day of the week. 'We started getting in smoked salmon for the Farmers' day. Seemed to sell well, so now we do smoked prawns from the Buckley Oysterage, smoked cod's roe, lobster, hand-dived scallops. You name it!' Kevin laughs. 'I mean, it's a load of old wank, but I'll take their money.'

He's even looking into setting up a stall in addition to the shop.

'I reckon I could sell the papers and lottery cards better out in the market. These guys'll pay up to six quid for an *Independent*. Can't argue with that.'

> **"It's a load of old wank, but I'll take their money."**

Lou Pembridge, 38 and Dan Gutherson, 40

Nice Buns! patisserie

> *"This year we're going to start selling chairs. Farmers' chairs, you know – artisan chairs. We get them from Ikea."*

Lou and Dan have been partners for twelve years. Until last year they had a multi-million pound fireplace business.

'Then came the recession,' says Lou with a practised stoicism. Dan takes up the story.

'First things to go in any period of difficulty are the luxuries. It was the same in the 30s.' It hasn't held them back, though. Lou immediately reached for the pinny, rolled up her sleeves and got going baking cakes.

'People will always love cakes, whatever the financial climate,' she says. And my word, they look good. Fairy cakes, muffins and Lou's trademark Nice Buns cupcakes.

'We sell about ten dozen of those every week,' says Dan, and I get the distinct impression that although these aren't hefty stone fireplaces, he still gets a buzz from the briskness of trade.

'Our margins are incredible,' says Lou. 'Around the fourth quarter of last year we were expecting to see a tailing-off, but if anything it went up. Well, it did go up. By £42,372. You don't happen to want any fireplaces, do you?'

For people like us
by **Josie Tulloh**, winner of the *A&M weekend* poetry competition

Take me out to the ring-road
Down beside the LaserQuest
A little slice of Arcadia
Out the back of the Toys R Us

'Cos there the horny hands of toil
Sell muddy veg and rape-seed oil
Brought straight from the farm
... for people like us!

There's ostrich steaks, smoked venison
And eggs with shit and feathers on;
There's cauliflowers
With gritty bits in between

If normal markets turn your head
Then wheel your Bugaboo here instead—
It's the furthest thing from *EastEnders*
    You've ever seen

Market! The Farmers' Market!
You drive here in the Volvo and you park it

Market! The Farmers' Market!
We find any old crap and sell it in a basket
Kumquats, bananas
And cheese from Southern France
Brought right here
    all freshly from the ground;
We've got cupcakes from our cupcake field
Just harvested this morning
They're yours
    a steal at six for thirty pound

Market! The Farmers' Market!
We're no more farmers than Morten Harket
But here are some fools and here's their
    money
The two are so easily parted
And soon we'll have enough to buy a farm

We've got flapjacks here
And sugared mice
Like a normal shop
    but not as nice
And pieces of ham
    just under the price of gold
Durian, walnuts, tangerines,
And little Batman figurines
All dug up this morning and ...
SOLD to the gentleman
    in the mustard cords

So if you drove from junctions two to four
And wondered what the queue was for
It's only the credulous masses
Of the urban middle classes;
In the carpark outside Discount Beds
We don't pay any overheads
So we make a small fortune every week
Just sat on our fat arses

Market! The Farmers' Market
You drive here in the Volvo and you park it

We're expanding to chairs this year
We get all the stuff from Ikea
Then give it some farmyard magic
Some scratches there, some chicken shit here
    And all of a sudden it's rather dear

Market! The Farmers' Market
We find any old crap and sell it in a basket
Hey, we've sold out already today
Must put some more tat on display
... and then go home

Market! The Farmers' Market!
We clear twenty grand by lunch
    and hit our target
'Cos here are the fools, here's their money
    the two are so easily parted
And soon we'll have enough ...
    Yes, soon we'll have enough ...
        Soon we'll have enough
To buy a farm

CHEESE 1·50 ↑

Risollo
w Rocket Salad + Truffle Oil £5

ORGanic Cox apples £1·90 a kilo pick + mix

Save me... Pro... 100% EGRADABLE

HANDMADE VEGGIE BURGERS

enly Halloumi OR Organic SuperVeg (VEGAN, WHEAT FREE)

- ON A LEAF £3·50
- IN A BUN £4·50
- ON A SALAD £5·50
- RAW TO COOK AT HOME £4·00

SAUCES ONE SPOON FREE, EXTRAS 50p

mato Salsa, Organic Hummus, Red Onion Jam

Kelly Boormann, 36
The Artisan Cyder Presse

Kelly pulls me into a jolly embrace and sets me down on her collapsible stool.

'What'll it be?' she asks misleadingly as she thrusts a warm cup of something divine-smelling into my hands. 'That's a mulled cider that I bring out for these mornings – I don't really sell it, it's just for me and my special friends.' She laughs winningly.

The stall itself groans under the weight of swollen gallon jerry-cans, all unlabelled and filled with a mysterious golden liquid.

'Thems are all cider – and thems are all perry,' sings Kelly in an Irish accent that wasn't there a moment ago. I would have expected, I say to her, that heavier items such as these would suffer in the absence of trolleys; surely shoppers don't want to lug something like that around for the morning?

'Ah, no,' says Kelly with a sweep of her hand, and for the first time I notice the swarm of teenagers sunning themselves on the grass, each of them nursing a jerry-can. It seems I'm quite wrong.

"Touch me, how can it be? Believe me, the sun always shines on TV. Hold me close to your heart – touch me and give all your love to me."

ONLY £20 PER JAR

Morten Harket, 51
Morten's Mustard

Morten knows all about local produce – he's from Norway! Already a veteran of the Oslo club scene with blues outfit Souldier Blue, he formed synth band a-ha in 1982 with pals Pal Waaktaar and Magne Furuholmen, enjoying international success with such hits as *Take On Me*, *Hunting High and Low*, and *The Sun Always Shines On TV*.

'Mustard is my life now,' says Morten as he unloads another crate of beautiful pots, accessorised with gingham lids so they resemble nothing so much as a little school nativity scene!

Ingredients

1.75 kg / 4 lb mussels without beards
1 garlic boat chopped so fine
2 shallot onions, chopped so fine also
15 g / ½ oz butter
bouquet garni of persil, thyme and bay
100 ml / 3.5 fl oz white wine or Apfel Funny
120 ml / 4 fl oz double cream
1 breasted tsp Morten's Lillehammer Mustard
fist of persil leaves, coarsely chopped
horny bread, for serving

MORTEN'S MUSSELS
'Wherever I am in the world I take a pot of Morten's Mustard so I can make this dish and feel like I'm right back in Kongsberg.'

Wash the mussels with heaps of cold water so that all mingey hair tassles and barnacles are gone.

Soften the garlic and shallot onions in the butter with the *bouquet garni* in a big pan for all the mussels at half capacity. Adding mussels and wine or Apfel Funny and the Morten's Lillehammer mustard.

Turn up heat, cover and steam in own juices for 3–4 minutes.

Shake crazy pan. Take away *bouquet garni* to the sea; add cream and persil.

Share with one you love.

Serves 2.

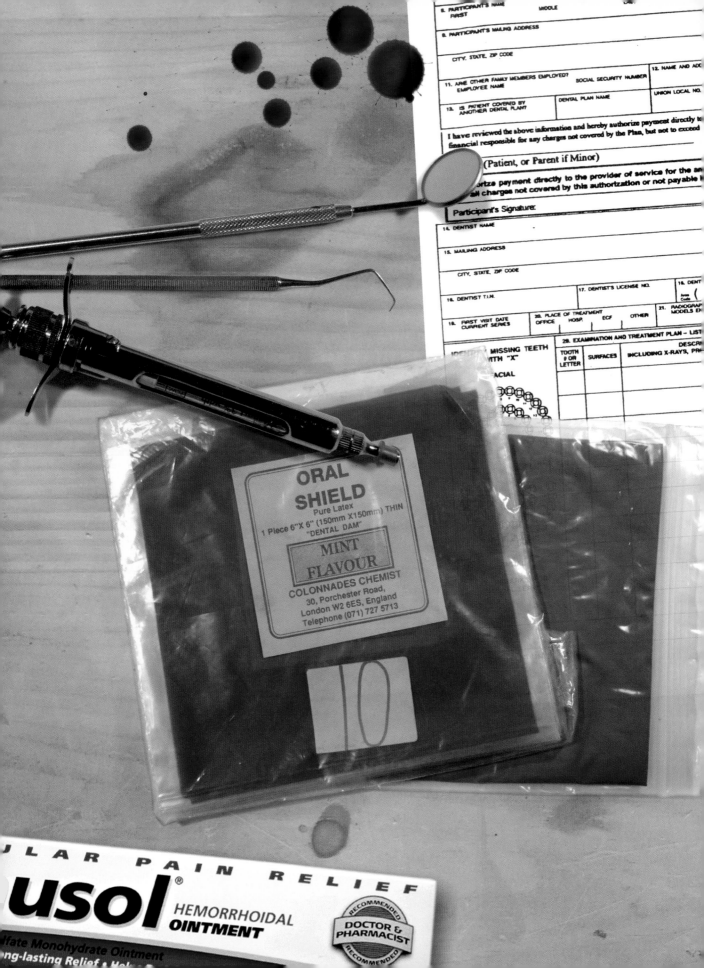

Hand in mouth: Getting inside the patient's head

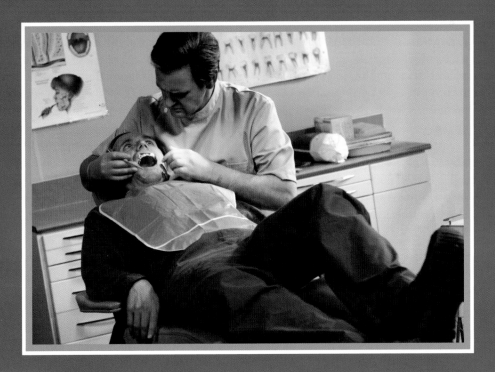

A Manual for Modern Consulting Rooms

5th Edition
FULLY REVISED

Hamish Dowland
DMD, MS, DDS, PhD

DENTI-PRAXIS

STORIES RELATING TO MY WIFE (SEXUAL)

STORIES RELATING TO MY WIFE (BODILY)

STORIES RELATING TO MY FAMILY (SEXUALLY SENSITIVE AREAS)

STORIES RELATING TO MY FAMILY (REVOLTING DISCLOSURES)

STORIES FROM MY ADOLESCENCE (SEXUAL)

STORIES FROM MY ADOLESCENCE (NAIVE)

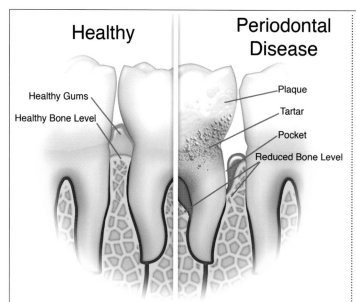

Healthy | **Periodontal Disease**

Healthy Gums
Healthy Bone Level

Plaque
Tartar
Pocket
Reduced Bone Level

FIGURE 18.

Surface characteristics and landmarks of the diseased periodontium

They're not showing you the best view here. If you peer down at one of these from 'tooth-side' you get an eyeful of something not unlike a torn dog's anus.

Cementum. If epithelium is the 'rabbit', then repair of cementum is the 'turtle' of periodontal wound healing. Not only is cementogenesis delayed in onset; it is also slow to exert its effect on the overall outcome of healing.

Palatal gingival. The gingival of the maxilla is continuous with the tissue of the palate. I'm not really firing on all cylinders today to be perfectly honest with you. My wife's developed a particularly virulent thrush – I wouldn't know if that's a more aggressive strain of the yeast or just a mild thrush that's been ignored and allowed to develop. God knows, we've all done it. Is that itch the dreaded 'T' word? Or is it just a build-up of smegma that I can probably work out with my thumbnail at a later juncture?

Honestly sometimes it's like a sherbert dib-dab down there. But a quick rinse under a cold tap (if you can stretch to that) will usually tidy up the pitch.

SELF-ASSESSMENT

Questions based on topics from the foregoing chapter. You may choose any number of responses (or follow directions in individual question rubric). Answers on p.446.

1   What is the most common reason for antibiotic failure in periodontal therapy?

❏ A   Inappropriate choice of antibiotics (the microorganism is not susceptible to the antibiotic of choice).

❏ B   Antibiotic antagonism (e.g. using bacteriocidal and bateriostatic antibiotics together).

❏ C   Impaired host defences.

❏ D   Patient noncompliance.

❏ E   Anyway, turns out she's pretty much 'off-games' for a bit.

2   What are other periodontal conditions that may require chemotherapeutic treatment?

❏ A   Vesiculobullous diseases

❏ B   Viral infections

❏ C   Needn't be the end of the world, of course. Plenty of other outlets for a red-blooded male. She'll probably want to be satisfied that the fungus hasn't spread to my penis before she pops the old fella in her mouth. Mind you, the good old mucogingival has always been my 'Port of Choice'.

STORIES FROM MY ADOLESCENCE (BESTIAL)

TALES FROM DENTAL CONFERENCES ('87–'95)

TALES FROM DENTAL CONFERENCES ('96–'04)

TALES FROM DENTAL CONFERENCES ('96–'04)

TALES FROM DENTAL CONFERENCES ('04–PRESENT EXCL. '05)

THE GREAT ROTHERHAM CONFERENCE 2005

3 What antibiotics are commonly used in periodontal therapy?

- ❏ **A** Amoxicillin (with or without clavulanic acid – Augmentin®)
- ❏ **B** Metronidazole
- ❏ **C** Ciprofloxacin
- ❏ **D** Azithromycin
- ❏ **E** But there are other options. Oh yes. Funny how it takes something like this to make you think more experimentally.

4 Which keratinocyte layers are apparent in fig. 4c.?

- ❏ **A** Stratum basale.
- ❏ **B** Stratum spinosum.
- ❏ **C** Stratum granulosum.
- ❏ **D** Stratum corneum.
- ❏ **E** And that doesn't mean I'm going straight for the Dirty Sanchez route!

5 How is force control achieved for a periodontal patient?

- ❏ **A** Occlusal adjustment.
- ❏ **B** Removable appliance therapy (e.g. bite-guards, Hawley appliances)
- ❏ **C** Fixed splints.
- ❏ **D** Orthodontic therapy.
- ❏ **E** Not ruling it out either of course.

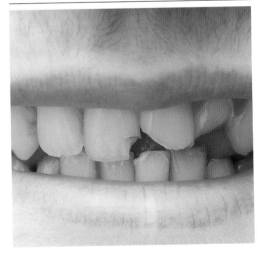

FIGURE 19a.
Our cat's on heat at the moment. They're very sexual beings, cats. I've got to be honest – I find the sight of her keening and rubbing herself against the furniture very engaging.

6 What are the indications for periodontal regeneration procedures?

- ❏ **A** The patient exhibits exemplary plaque control both before and after regenerative therapy.
- ❏ **B** The patient does not smoke.
- ❏ **C** There is occlusal stability of the teeth at the regenerative site.
- ❏ **D** Osseous defects are vertical, with bone walls remaining.
- ❏ **E** There's the breasts, of course – wonderfully sensitive. And in my wife's case there's enough there to achieve an incredibly satisfactory purchase. And what's nice about that is it's very much a mutual thing.

7 How is pericoronitis treated?

- ❏ **A** After anaesthesia, clean out debris under the operculum with irrigation or ultrasonics.
- ❏ **B** Occlusal adjustment or removal of the opposing molar.
- ❏ **C** Antibiotics, usually penicillin, are indicated if there are systemic factors.
- ❏ **D** But there's all sorts of games you can play. You know, to draw out the experience. These can be a lot of fun.

8 What materials are available for periodontal plastic surgical procedures?

- ❏ **A** Autogenous gingiva, connective tissue and/or bone.
- ❏ **B** Allograft connective tissue substitutes (Alloderm®) or bone grafting materials.
- ❏ **C** Xenograft bone fill materials.
- ❏ **D** There's the old 'I climb into the bath/she straddles me/wait for nature to take its course' chestnut. There's something deeply erotic about a good old hosing with warm urine. Who'd have thought!

9 What types of initial incisions are made in periodontal flap surgery?

- ❏ **A** Sulcular incision.
- ❏ **B** Marginal Incision.
- ❏ **C** Submarginal Incision.
- ❏ **D** And if you want to take that to its natural extreme you can always go for the coffee table option.

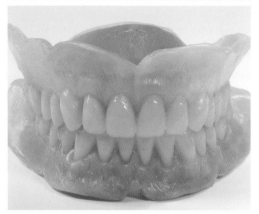

FIGURE 19b.
Amazing how nature is just full of sex isn't it? I was chopping logs the other day and I found a bit of wood that was Y-shaped where two branches grew out and I swear it was like a perfect wooden sculpture of the pudendum. I kept that one. It's in our bedroom now.

10. **What methods of periodontal flap repair are available?**

☐ A Replacement of tissue by dissimilar tissue.

☐ B Reattachment of connective tissue.

☐ C Healing with epithelium and connective tissue on a previously diseased root surface.

☐ D Regeneration/replacement with histologically and functionally identical tissues.

☐ E I guess it works like a glass-bottomed boat in reverse, really. You underneath looking up. Her above, coiling one down. One for the biologists, that one, I guess, although – heck, I found it weirdly arousing.

11. **Which factors influence the need for osseous surgery?**

☐ A The number of remaining walls.

☐ B The depth of the defect.

☐ C The proximity of the defect to important anatomical landmarks.

☐ D The amount of bone that will be removed to achieve positive bony architecture.

☐ E My wife and I have discussed getting piercings. You know, intimate ones.

12. **What are the common periodontal emergencies?**

☐ A Acute herpetic gingivostomatitis.

☐ B Necrotizing ulcerative gingivitis.

☐ C Periodontal abscess.

☐ D Periocoronitis.

☐ E For a number of years I had what they call a Prince Albert. That is, a ring through the nut of the penis.

13. **How is the diagnosis of the emergency condition determined?**

☐ A Is the problem acute or chronic?

☐ B Is the pain dull, sharp or throbbing?

☐ C Is the tooth sensitive to biting or percussion?

☐ D Has there been any drainage from the swelling or bad taste?

☐ E Has the patient been eating popcorn or nuts?

☐ F Is the patient febrile?

☐ F Is the pulp vital?

☐ G It's said to enhance the stimulation of the gland, although I'll be honest it did nothing for me.

14. **How may the sequence of events in periodontal wound healing be interrupted?**

☐ A Epithelial cells begin to proliferate at wound margins.

☐ B Fibroblasts begin to proliferate after day 2 with evidence of collagen synthesis.

☐ C Osteoclasts appear in the wound.

☐ D Made my old chap look like something off 'Rainbow'.

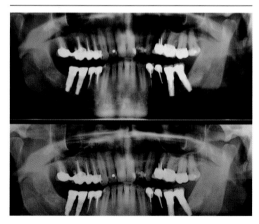

FIGURE 19c.
You'll even find nature's little peep-shows in people's mouths. In the course of my day job I've been titillated many times by the shapes I've found in patients' gingiva. I love this job.

CHAPTER 5

Take a seat:
"The Doctor's Friend"

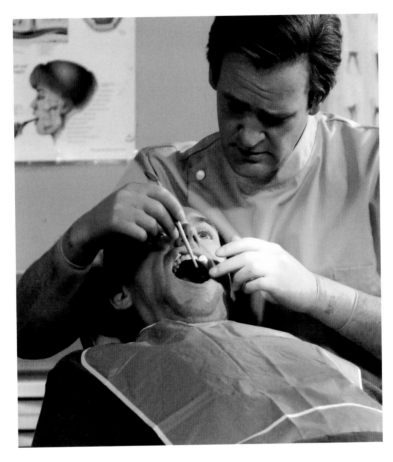

The University Of Michigan published a report in 2007 demonstrating the stress levels experienced by patients in the dentist's chair. Much of this distress – as was shown with use of placebo and control experiments – was entirely in the mind of the subject.

There are several ways to put a patient at ease – the most obvious is what I call 'The Doctor's Friend': the bedside manner. I find a homely anecdote or revelation quickly lets your patient know that you are a human being too!

Just the other day I was reminded of how human I am. I was finishing off a – how can I put this delicately? – a toiletry evacuation. A dump. And while giving it the old wiperoo downstairs I must have dislodged a hanger-on.

Anyway, because it comes out at perfect body temperature it doesn't always make its presence felt, if you catch me. Moments later I unwittingly must have put my hand through my hair or something because I looked in the mirror when I arrived at work and

STORIES FROM MY ADOLESCENCE (BESTIAL)

TALES FROM DENTAL CONFERENCES ('87–'95)

TALES FROM DENTAL CONFERENCES ('96–'04)

TALES FROM DENTAL CONFERENCES ('96–'04)

TALES FROM DENTAL CONFERENCES ('04–PRESENT EXCL. '05)

THE GREAT ROTHERHAM CONFERENCE 2005

Taking Off

By Capt. Jack 'Biffy' Wentworth, R.A.F.

Flying in wartime belongs to the Yoot, and the Yoot of the British Empire is like found a new heritage in the air. To the Royal Air Force and to the Fleet Air Arm of the Royal Navy the bredren of the British Empire is flocking in their thousands, from Capetown to London, Liverpool to Melbourne, Brisbane to Toronto, Auckland to Mauritius. They wants to fly for Britain, isn't it.

From countless aerodromes in England and Canada, great powerful engines is roaring a symphony of speed and a thousand whirring propellors tell the tale of impatient ghetto at the controls, learning to fly and shit.

Every day all over the Empire, air cadets is aloft in their training aircraft qualifying for the proudest possession of any British youth of to-day—the cream white wings of the Royal Air Force or the golden wings of the Fleet Air Arm. Standard.

Not all the gold in the world, nor all the influence can like buy you a pair of those wings and entitle you to wear them, but hear me now, any lad of 18 and upwards can earn them, be he rich or on free dinners, and once he has them up, me fam, no one can take them from him.

Let us follow two boys who have just turned 18 and who have joined the R.A.F. and the Fleet Air Arm respectively. We'll call them Choon and K-man. K-man has always been mad about speed (he was riding his brother's motor cycle when he was 16) and he wants bad

to be a Spitfire pilot, hurtling through the air at like 400 miles per hour. He enters the R.A.F. through the only door open in wartime—the ranker's door. He becomes an Aircraftsman Second Class isn't it.

At the Initial Training Wing, where he spends two months, he doesn't see a aeroplane! He's too busy getting baked, crunked, and hitting the switches with some butterface from the Supply Room, but if he keeps his shit together he finds himself at the Elementary Flying Training School and the Big Day comes when he climbs into a "Tiger Moth" and goes aloft for his first dual instruction in actual flying, no bullshit.

Of course, a Tiger isn't a Spitfire, being something like 300 miles an hour slower than our 1941 Spitfires, but K-man doesn't mind. He's just happy to be airborne, fo sho.

Big Day No. 2 comes when K-man is told by his instructor: "She's all yours, sonny. Bring her back in one piece!" Just like that!

With his heart in his mouth, but with a gleam of determination in his eye, K-man opens the Tiger's throttle and it sails into the air for all the world like a kite caught in a gust of wind. K-man will show 'em. This is the chance he has been wainting for.

He climbs up to 1,000 feet, straightens his trainer-aircraft out and feels so scare that he nearly shit hisself.

FOR, AS THEY SPEAK ...

Grandpère!
'Ave you ever seen
zo many planes?!

MEANWHILE, AT R.A.F. BIGGIN HILL ...

MEANWHILE ...

39

TO BE CONTINUED ON PAGE 185 ...

DIG FOR VICTORY & SHIT

Welcome to Brady's!

We are a friendly family restaurant, based in the Bristol area since 1998.
Take some time to browse the menu!
If you need anything just ask one of the bears!*

Bears have no concept of mealtimes! They simply eat as and when they are hungry, or when an opportunity presents itself. So the idea of a meal part way between breakfast and lunch would be meaningless!

Pawprints shown nowhere near actual, potentially lethal size

Brunch

Honey Bear Pancakes
£3.95

Get your day off to a glorious start with our delicious wholewheat pancakes drenched with sumptuous runny honey.

Fruit Bear Yoghurt with Granola
£3.50

Take the healthy option with this lip-smackingly nutritious bowl of organic oat clusters, pumpkin seeds and whole hazelnuts, smothered in whole-milk yoghurt.

Sloth Bear Lazy Brunch
£4.95

Take a load off with this Brady's special: a full English breakfast with organic farm-sourced pork sausage, golden hash browns, two eggs any style and choice of beans or button mushroom side. Comes with home-baked wheat toast with butter and preserves. And here's the kicker: no time limit on the table!

Bear facts!

Look out for these symbols on the menu:

Hot and spicy Great for vegetarians May contain nuts

Healthy option approved by the British Heart Foundation

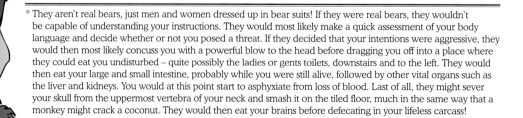

---

* They aren't real bears, just men and women dressed up in bear suits! If they were real bears, they wouldn't be capable of understanding your instructions. They would most likely make a quick assessment of your body language and decide whether or not you posed a threat. If they decided that your intentions were aggressive, they would then most likely concuss you with a powerful blow to the head before dragging you off into a place where they could eat you undisturbed – quite possibly the ladies or gents toilets, downstairs and to the left. They would then eat your large and small intestine, probably while you were still alive, followed by other vital organs such as the liver and kidneys. You would at this point start to asphyxiate from loss of blood. Last of all, they might sever your skull from the uppermost vertebra of your neck and smash it on the tiled floor, much in the same way that a monkey might crack a coconut. They would then eat your brains before defecating in your lifeless carcass!

Starters & Sharing

 Asian Bear Spare Ribs

£5.95

Achingly tender slow-braised hand-reared pork ribs marinaded in five spice sauce. Perfect finger food for families and friends. Or, even better: have a whole portion to yourself!

 **European Bear Bruschetta**

£4.95

Four slices of home-baked rustic bread dripping with farm-churned, full-cream butter and a zingy salsa of luscious vine-ripened Italian tomatoes and fresh chopped herbs. Plenty to share!

Add Olive Tapenade: £1.50

Mexican Grizzly Bear Rancheros

£3.95

Brady's unique take on the Mexican country classic *Huevos Rancheros*. Two large organic hen's eggs cradled in a mouth-watering nest of twice-fried potato shavings and smothered in delicious melted Monterey Jack cheese.

Mains

Brady's Grizzly Burgers

£9.25 *cub size: £4.95*

8 oz of flame-grilled prime Angus beef cooked to order on a home-baked whole-wheat poppy-seed bun, with a succulent helping of cos lettuce, beef tomato, red onion, Brady's pickle, mayonnaise and barbecue relish, accompanied by melt-in-the-mouth skin-on fries.

Toppings: £1.10 each

Choose from bacon, mature cheddar, mushrooms, grated beetroot, fried egg, flash-fried onions, guacamole, hummus and jalapeños.

Russian Bear Chicken Kiev

£12.95 *cub size: £6.65*

A pecorino-and-parmesan-crumbed organic chicken breast with sensational melting garlic and herb butter, accompanied with skin-on new potato mash, market-fresh rocket and oven-roasted lemon.

 Dolomite Bear Meatballs On Fettuccine

£9.85 *cub size: £4.95*

Slow-braised meatballs in Brady's original spicy cajun sauce with peppers, smoky paprika, red onions and organic vine-ripened tomatoes.

Desserts

Polar Bear Ice Creams

£4.95

Two generous scoops of homemade organic ice cream, topped with the sauce of your dreams. Choose from chunky choc, mint choc, pistachio, vanilla, cream caramel, butterscotch, or funky coconut ice cream, and top with marshmallow magic, hot choc, frothy toffee or millionaire sauce.

Giant Panda Chocolate Cake with White Chocolate Ripple
£4.80

Definitely one for those with a sweet tooth! A rich, moist chocolate sponge cake ladled with a very vanilla cream filling and topped off with exquisite white chocolate. Ask for two forks!

Giant Pandas, along with the majority of bear species, cannot metabolise the chemical *theobromine*, present in chocolate! If a Giant Panda were to eat a slice of chocolate cake of the size served here it would quickly develop stomach cramps, and die, most likely from a heart attack.

Cinnamon Bear Apple Cake

£4.50

Organic Bramley apples spiced with just a pinch of cinnamon and baked in delicious slow-baked homemade shortcrust pastry.
Add a dollop of Brady's ice cream: £1.95

Blue Bear Slushy
£4.50

A real favourite with the kids, and healthy too! A natural blueberry slushy topped with a raspberry, strawberry and cranberry crush.

You might think there is no such thing as either a 'Cinnamon Bear' or a 'Blue Bear' and that we made up the names to suit the menu. If so, you would be wrong.

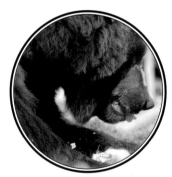

The Real Brady

Brady was a 700lb Grizzly Bear who was responsible for eight fatal attacks on humans in the remote settlement of King Cove, Alaska, during a seven-month period in 1995. Brady had been feeding at the town dump and lost his fear of humans, and simultaneously began to associate them with food. When the town mayor insisted that the dump be fenced off to prevent Brady and other bears from feeding, Brady was starved of his regular nutrient source and began a reign of terror, dragging people from their homes at night, mauling passers-by in broad daylight, and on one occasion even scaling the walls of an elementary school and eating one of the teachers.

A Word About Our Charity

Fifty pence from every Grizzly Burger sold at Brady's goes to our charity **Bear Action** for the human victims of bear attacks. Every year countless people lose their lives in encounters with bears, usually because they have failed to respect the bears' natural habitat. Through a programme of education and conservation, we at Brady's hope to be able to avoid bear attacks in the future, and to provide urgently needed medical care to people suffering from bear maimings and maulings.

The following victims were too late to receive our help. Let's hope others are more fortunate!

Hannah Charles was attacked and killed by a 750lb Polar Bear on the Antarctic peninsula in June 2009 while

she was in transit to join the British Antarctic Expedition as a field scientist measuring ice core samples. The bear overturned a motor-powered sledge carrying Hannah and three others, and dragged her struggling body 500 yards before drowning her in the ice-cold waters of the Antarctic sea. Her corpse was never recovered.

Lorraine Hachette-Brown, seen here holidaying in Yosemite National Park in October 2008, was dragged from

her tent at night by a full-grown male Grizzly after he scented food from her campsite. The bear mauled her in full view of her fiancé, Stephen Marchlake, before killing her by pressing one of his front paws on her windpipe. The bear then pursued Stephen for some 800 yards, before he had a lucky escape when a Ranger's vehicle sounded its horn and the animal retreated. The bear was subsequently captured and destroyed.

Amy Elvin was attacked and killed by a Black Bear while jogging in a wooded area near Quebec City, Quebec, Can-

ada. It is unusual for a bear attack to occur so close to a large city, and the reasons for it remain undetermined. A Black Bear was subsequently trapped by Wildlife rangers near the location of the incident but it was determined that this was not the bear responsible for the fatal mauling. The coroner's report suggested that she was able to get away from the bear after its initial attack, but that it caught up with her and delivered a fatal blow to the back of her neck.

Ian Mandy made the mistake of repeatedly feeding bears near his home in White River, Colorado, despite warnings by

wildlife officials. In March 2009 he began feeding a 10-month-old Black Bear cub who had been wounded in a fight with a larger juvenile bear. The larger bear approached his house one evening later that same month, and Mandy was attempting to scare it away when it clubbed through the screened porch, dragged him off and killed him.

Sandra Teviott and her husband **Christopher** were hiking in Romania when they chanced upon a 500lb

European Brown Bear feeding on a wild pig kill. Sandra was killed instantly by a cuff from the bear's paw; Christopher survived the initial mauling but died in hospital three days later from blood poisoning.

Cindy Morris, 8, was holidaying with her grandparents in Prince George, British Columbia, Canada, when, in an

extremely unusual attack, a 750lb Grizzly Bear overturned their recreation vehicle and dragged her off into a thicket of poison ivy. Unable to reach her granddaughter through the poison ivy, Cindy's grandmother attempted to scare the animal off by sounding the vehicle's horn. Her grandfather then fired several shots at the bear, to no discernible effect, while the animal sat on the child's face leisurely eating her guts.

Brady says:
'Bon appetit! Enjoy your meal!'

Brady's Tipping Policy

Boudoir D'Amour

The Winter Collection

introduced by our experts
Yvonne Hammond and Lisa Varey

CAT# PCR124
Leelee Ouvert
☐ ROYAL
■ JET
SIZES 28–44"

£45 +£3.95 P&P

Leelee Ouvert Panties

Yvonne: 'Ouvert'. That's French for 'open', isn't it?

Lisa: That's right, Yvonne – your worst fears are confirmed. God help us.

Yvonne: What are these for? The incontinent? Where's the pleasure in a great draft blowing around your undercarriage?

Lisa: It's beyond me. But I'm a tights woman. I like when winter comes and I can pull on a big pair of woolly ones.

Yvonne: Again – £45 for bit of tiny cloth. Somebody's making a mint.

CAT# BR456
Desirée
■ MIDNIGHT
■ HUSSY
☐ NUDE
SIZES XS, S,M,L,XL

£75 +£4.95 P&P

Desirée Quarter-Cup Fun Bra

Lisa: What's fun about a bra? For goodness' sake. I do wish men would grow up. This one certainly isn't up to much. It's about as supportive as Yvonne's ex-husband.

Yvonne: I mean, what's the point of it? You might as well walk round with your jumper over your head.

Lisa: £75. That's a week's shop for you, isn't it Yvonne? (She goes to Waitrose.)

Yvonne: Only because they do Taylor's Tea there – which they don't at our Tescos.

CAT# PCR124
Leelee Ouvert
■ CHERRY
■ EBONY
SIZES 28–44"

£49 +£3.95 P&P

Miranda Tie-side Panties

Lisa: Apparently you pull at them and they come undone 'in one graceful move'.

Yvonne: How useful.

Lisa: Your ex-husband would have struggled with the knots, wouldn't he?

Yvonne: In 17 years of marriage I could never get him to untie his shoelaces. He'd just pull them off and push them back on again. His shoes always wore out at the back. He was a lazy oaf.

Lisa: Who on earth wants separate knickers for the bedroom anyway? All that faffing about. Where do people find the time?

Somerset Waspie

Lisa: You thought it was something to do with your holidays, didn't you, Yvonne?

Yvonne: I don't want to talk about it. Mrs Senior, who does a lot of my alterations, had a terrible accident when she sat on a wasp in Taunton and got stung on her vagina. It was no laughing matter I can assure you.

CAT# WS024
Somerset

- BRUISE
- BISQUE
- ACE of SPADES

SIZES XXS, XS, S, M

£185
+£9.95 P&P

£60
+£5.95 P&P

CAT# LBY1100
Yolanda

- LILAC
- SHEER
- BATTER

SIZES L, XL, XXL

Yolanda Full Brief

Lisa: At first I thought: 'finally, something someone would actually want to wear'.

Yvonne: I know – something big and comfortable.

Lisa: But look again. They're see-through.

Yvonne: Oh, for God's sake. It's more like something you'd buy onions in.

Lisa: You couldn't wear those, could you Yvonne? Not with your pubic region. It would look like a bale of hay.

Yvonne: I don't believe in depilation.

Lisa: You should have seen her face when I explained what a Brazilian was.

Yvonne: Women are their own worst enemies.

£29
+£2.95 P&P

Boudoir d'Amour Massage Oils

Lisa: Better for doing a wood floor with. I used these on some scrapes from a piano stool and it came up like new.

£25
+£5.95 P&P

CAT# ACC224
Razzle

- RUBY
- LIVID

SIZES one size fits all

Razzle Pasties

Yvonne: Not the Cornish variety, unfortunately. These are things you stick on your nipples, apparently.

Lisa: Imagine asking for these in Greggs.

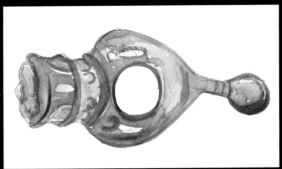

CAT# CLIT2335A
Energiser
□ CUTTLEFISH
□ AUREOLE
SIZES made to measure

£19
+£1.95 P&P

Energiser Clit Ring

Yvonne: I genuinely had no idea what this was for.

Lisa: You could use it for holding all the wires together round the back of the telly.

CAT# MAT0045
Aphrodite
■ BIG MOMMA
□ LACTOSE
■ JELLY
SIZES 36–58" BUST

£139
+£8.95 P&P

Aphrodite
Maternity Bra & Brief Set for sensual play while pregnant

Yvonne: As if.

CAT# PLY44024
Intrigue
□ HITHER
■ DAMNATION
■ CONVENT
SIZES one size fits all

03456/045 **'Sorbet'**
Ladies Dressing Gown heavy viscose/co...
£1...

Now you're talkin...

Intrigue Playsuit

Lisa: Playsuit! Who would that suit, I ask you?

Yvonne: You could drape on some leftover spaghetti and get the same effect. And edible items are always popular. With the more cheapskate of our erotic adventurers.

Martin Christie

Window Cleaning Solutions Ltd.

Cleaning windows and providing possible solutions to the world's intractable social, political and economic problems since 1986

FEDERATION OF WINDOW CLEANERS
FWC

ALL OUR STAFF ARE FULLY TRAINED

CONSERVATORIES & GREENHOUSES

ABOUT US

Since 1986 Christie Window Cleaning has become one of the leading providers of window cleaning services in the Northumberland area.

Our fully trained, uniformed personnel will do everything to ensure you receive 100% customer satisfaction.

We use many different methods of window cleaning and have an impeccable safety record.

Our customer base ranges from domestic properties to churches, offices, retail parks, family homes and many leading NGOs, Intelligence Agencies and Departments of State.

'Christie Window Cleaning always give an excellent and reliable service'
—**Carol Hatchard**, managing director, 'A Cut Above' hair and beauty salons

25% NEW CUSTOMER DISCOUNT

TRUTH & RECONCILIATION

OUR LOYAL CUSTOMERS

Examples of some of our regular satisfied clients:

* Bentley's supermarkets
* Whittlewell Motor Group
* Melton Dunn Construction Ltd
* Laura's Bakery, Newton Aycliffe
* United Nations Initiative on Conflict Resolution and Ethnicity

'Christie Window Cleaning can be relied upon for a visionary approach and open-minded exploration of some of the world's most difficult and persistent conflict situations.'

—Steven Wainright, Demos Think-Tank

INFLATION

In 1963 Milton Friedman proclaimed that 'Inflation is always and everywhere a monetary problem.' If this is the case then why does society not have sound media of exchange via its monetary system? We at Martin Christie Window Cleaning Services believe the answer is simple: the truth is inflation is always and everywhere a political phenomenon. A monetary authority produces inflation and that authority is itself political. With one political arrangement, money may be stable but with another it can just as easily be productive of deflation. A society's inflation and deflation cannot be understood or addressed without understanding its political forces. Until this nettle is grasped inflation will remain a chronic ailment of all economies.

* Water-fed pole ladderless window cleaning
* Traditional services using chamois leather and vinegar water
* Signs, facias and cladding
* Pressure washing
* uPVC cleaning
* Conservatory roof cleaning
* Non-directive all-party negotiations arranged and supervised
* Promotion of interfaith dialogue
* Gutters cleared

FREQUENTLY ASKED QUESTIONS

Q. CAN YOU WASH WINDOWS THAT HAVE WOODEN FRAMES?

A. Yes, as long as your window frames are in prime condition. We don't wash them down like we would uPVC ones, however.

Q. WE HAVE LEADED WINDOWS. CAN YOU WASH THEM?

A. Absolutely. No problems at all.

Q. IS IT POSSIBLE TO FIND A SOLUTION TO THE BORDER ISSUES TROUBLING SOUTHERN THAILAND?

A. If Malaysia is in earnest about not allowing Pattani separatist sympathisers to aid the disruptive elements in the three southern provinces then there is no reason why a lasting peace should not be found in the region.

Call us about special rates for pensioners, UB40 and unrecognised nation states.

089994 232323

The Origins of ...

... circus skills
workshops

... binge
drinking

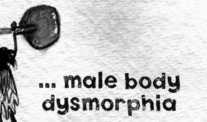

... male body
dysmorphia

... water-cooler moments

... massive golf sales

... trying to get your hair cut like a celebrity's

... chugging

... 24hr kebab shops

The Origins of Lifestyle Technology

Newly discovered artefacts from the Stone Age epoch revolutionise
our understanding of our hominid ancestors

meStone

Granite with quartz inclusions
340g approx.
Middle Palaeolithic era (120,000–24,000 years ago)
Acquired with support of the Young Friends of the Museum Director
and the Betty E. Clark Memorial Fund

Its handy size and clean lines must have
been part of the appeal, but it was the
amazing versatility of the meStone that
ensured its adoption as a must-have tool
by all progressive Neanderthals.

Applications were almost limitless,
including hitting things, throwing at
things, and smashing things such as the
skulls of small birds and mammals.

Two meStones could easily be docked
and banged together rhythmically, making
it the first portable music player.

There is also evidence that a sharpening
app may have emerged during the early
Upper Palaeolithic, allowing the meStone
to be used for carving, skinning and even
depilation.

mePebble

Banded gneiss
100–250g approx.
Upper Palaeolithic era (35,000–10,000 years ago)
Brabbins Bequest *in lieu* of taxes

Eventually the meStone was superseded as users across the plains of
Northern Europe upgraded to the mePebble.

Retaining and building on the functionality of the meStone Classic, it is
thought the mePebble, being more portable, was better suited to primitive
peoples kept on the move by climactic variability and, concurrently,
developing an increased appetite for less utilitarian activities such as
skipping their mePebble over ponds and 'stone-washing' their garments.

Also available in a range of funky new colours.

Now on show First Floor Prehistory Annexe

meRock
Metamorphic basalt
52kg approx.
Lower Palaeolithic era (1,000,000–100,000 years ago)
Gift of Bill and Melinda Gates

Our most recent discovery, the original meRock pre-dates the meStone by eons. Although undoubtedly important in its time, palaeontologists believe its massive weight may have limited its range of applications.

INSIDE THE BOX.

You might think:
"it's just a bit of thin plastic,
it'll be fine"

You might think:
"leaflets and stuff will fall
out and blow everywhere"

But if you put supplements in the
paper recycling without removing the
plastic sleeve ... the next sleeve you
see could be on a prison uniform.

TAKE THE WRAPPER OFF.
OR TAKE THE RAP.

TOLPUDDLE MARTYRS

Above: Tolpuddle Martyr George Loveless, an inspiring speaker. Clearly on one if you look at his eyes.

Left: The famous Tolpuddle sycamore today: Can you spot Jason's mate Andy at work in his 'office'?

Just outside Dorchester on the road to Poole lies the small Dorset village of Tolpuddle. It was under a giant sycamore tree here in Tolpuddle that English trade unionism was born in the 1830s. Jason's mate Andy lives in Poole – he's always good for a couple of grams.

In 1830 the wage of an agricultural labourer was nine shillings, the next year it was lowered to eight, and then seven. By 1834 labourers were facing a six-shilling wage. Andy's wage is 45 quid a gram. Don't know if you call that a wage but he lives with his mum still so it's kind of all profit. She's diamond – you'd never believe she was like fifty-seven. She came to Reading with us last year and was last one to bed both nights and started a fight in The Water Rats!

To contest their dwindling wages a small group of Tolpuddle

workers set up the Friendly Society of Agricultural Labourers. The Society became extremely popular and thanks to the inspiring oratory of George Loveless, one of its founders, its membership grew and grew. Jason has started a club in town – their membership's doing pretty well too. It's great, they've got like two floors and because it's private members only they don't have to stick to council rules so there's touching and everything.

By the following spring the Society agreed that its members would not accept work of any kind for under ten shillings. This was not popular with the authorities who instantly ordered the arrest of six men: James Brine, James Hammett, George Loveless, James Loveless (George's brother), Thomas Standfield (George's brother-in-law) and Thomas' son, John Standfield. Jason and I have also

been arrested a couple of times, but we're always careful to make sure we're not holding anything beyond personal use and so far we've kept a clean sheet, bar a couple of cautions.

Although their trade union was completely legal, the six were duly arrested on an archaic technicality relating to naval law and brought for trial at the Dorchester Assizes. They were all found guilty as charged and sentenced to seven years

Van Diemen's Land, now called Tasmania, where some of the Martyrs ended up. These days the club scene there is picking up.

The shelter built as a memorial to the Martyrs in 1934. We were shown the sights by some local sorts. Being on the telly always helps with a casual hookup when you're out of town.

The Martyrs' achievements in standing up for the workers still inspire people to this day.

transportation to the penal colony in New South Wales, Australia; not for anything they had done but as an example to others. We're going to Australia next year for our expedition – I can't wait. Two weeks in total, five days in Sydney then on to the Gold Coast, two days in Alice Springs and the rest of the time is our own. We're going to Razzamatazz in Canberra – or Five Floors Of Whores as I believe they call it. I am going to get in there and do my NUTS.

The case aroused huge interest all over the country and led to a mass demonstration in London in April 1834 when 35 Unions gathered to present a petition of 200,000 signatures to the prime minister, Lord Melbourne. Haven't yet spoken to my Melbourne connection so that part of the schedule is looking a bit light.

Five of the men were transported to Australia; George Loveless was delayed through illness, then he too was sent away, although in his case it was to Tasmania. Don't worry though, my friends, there'll be nothing 'loveless' about Melbourne by the time we get out there. Because we are going to get so pissed and take SO many drugs and shag SOOOOOOO many fine Ozzy ladies, we will be ON THE FREAKIN' NEWS. Deedle-ee dee dee, deedle-eedle-eedle-eedle-eedle-ee dee dee dibber diddle-ing-ting!

Public pressure led to the men being pardoned by the King. Months passed before the news of the pardon reached the Australian authorities. The martyrs didn't return to England until three years after their notorious trial. And when they finally did, their reception was muted owing to the poor

health of the King. WEEE AARE THE SHAAAAAAGPIONS MY FRIENDS! AND WE'LL KEEEEEP TAAAKING CHAAAARLIE TILL THE END!!! NOOO TIME FOR LOOOOOOOSERZ COZ WEEE AAAARE THE SHAAAAAAAAAAAAAAGPIONS – OF THE WORLD.

One of the six convicted men – James Hammett – remained in Tolpuddle in relative anonymity, but pressure from disgruntled local landowners forced the other five to seek new lives elsewhere, which they did – very happily – in London, Ontario, in Canada.

During this last piece on the Tolpuddle Martyrs there have been several moments where I have made references to alcohol, intoxicating substances and sexual matters, some of which were offensive. I now realise that when these lapses occurred it was wrong and I would like to say to you all that I'm sorry. I have let myself down, my colleagues down, but above all I have let you, the reader, down.

The grave of James Hammett, who never left Tolpuddle, not even on a gap year.

A memorial erected by Tolpuddle Council to commemorate the great achievements of the Martyrs. Probably a nice spot for a quiet puff when the pubs kick out.

Expedition to Amsterdam!

We all had a great adventure in Amsterdam. This unique city is only a couple of hours away but filled with history and surprises.

The city was originally called 'Amstellerdam' which means 'dam in the River Amstell'.

It was founded in the twelfth century and soon became one of the most important ports in Europe.

Amsterdam is famous for its canals, and is often called 'The Venice of the North'.

There are over one hundred kilometres of canals and 1,500 bridges.

Cannabis is legal in Amsterdam. This is one of the city's famous 'brown cafés' where, unlike in England, PG Tips isn't the strongest thing on the menu!

There was lots to choose from. In the end Jason ordered a 'space cake' – a cookie made with liquid THC – while Katy and Andrew opted for a 'hot knife', where a small quantity of resin is vapourised using a heated pair of knives, then consumed using a sort of funnel.

This is Jason being arrested by a Dutch policeman in the Van Gogh Museum after having a psychotic episode.

The Museum has the largest collection of Van Gogh's paintings and drawings in the world.

Jason somehow shook the policeman off and hid in the gift shop of Anne Frank's house until his eyes started working again.

Anne hid here herself for two years and a month until she was anonymously betrayed to the Nazis.

Katy was really wasted so Andrew took her to the Red Light district to cheer her up. A basic 'F&S' costs about 50 Euros, no matter how attractive the girl is. Andrew wanted a few extras so ended up paying 150.

Luckily the girl he chose, Harmony, was also able to sell him a couple of grams of coke.

This is the Rijksmuseum. We never made it here.

We now realise that when these things happened in Amsterdam they were wrong. We appreciate that while in Amsterdam we were there as your representatives and therefore we should apologise to you. We let ourselves down, we let you down, but most of all we let the programme down. And if we don't go through with this shameless apology they will almost certainly sack us.

SHIT .... I FORGOT TO
PUT THE BINS OUT

INTENSITY

Simon Vickers Can't Do Thursday · He's Flying To Düsseldorf
'Stressed' Backwards is 'Desserts' · This Has Not Been Used Enough In Greetings Cards
Paul McCartney Never Carries A Hanky · Indoor Fireworks Are Seldom Exciting
If You Touch The Bit Below Your Nose You'll Stop Most Sneezes
The Starters In Greek Restaurants Are Usually Enough

A

ENDORSED BY LEADING BUSINESSMEN

IMAGINE

Ashley Cole Couldn't Tie His Own Shoelaces Till He Was Twelve · Glasgow's Miles Better
Dawn From Accounts Is Thinking About Going To Garsington · Tommy Steele Hates Wednesdays
Donkeys Only See In Reds And Yellows · Old VHS Machines Are Now Worth A Fortune
The Wombles Are Worth A Second Listen · Lake Como Is Getting a Bit Overcrowded
Anyone Can Afford To Go Skiing · Enid Blyton Was A Rotten Mother

B

HASSLE-FREE RETURNS. JUST PHONE US WITHIN 30 DAYS.

INSPIRING

You Should Put Ammonia On A Bee Sting And Vinegar On a Wasp Sting
Jerry Cottle's Dad Was A Stockbroker · Syd Little Can't Say 'Tangerine'
If You Fast For A Week Your Breath Smells Of Acetate · You'll Never Get A Dog In A Bath
Not All Country House Hotels Are Very Nice · Lady Gaga Sometimes Goes Too Far
Ricky Gervais Could Lighten Up A Bit · Alain De Botton Will Always Raise A Smile

NEW

As LOW as
£5.99
each

MOTIVATIONAL POSTERS

Generate a creative buzz around your watercooler or smoking shelter

- Beautiful images inspire
- Original insights feed the Thinking Environment
- Hammer home the Three I's
- Laminated for wipe-clean convenience

Vagueinc® Order Code#	Description	Price Each	
		1	3
(A) G24-1650164	INTENSITY	£6.99	£5.99
(B) G24-1650165	IMAGINE	£6.99	£5.99
(C) G24-1650166	INSPIRING	£7.99	£6.99

FREE HANDY BISCUIT TOWER
with every poster order

Quote Offer Code BISCUIT TOWER when ordering

stereo

FLP203 ★ LONG PLAY 33⅓ R.P.M

FIRST TRUMP

PARENTAL
ADVISORY
EXQUISITE CONTENT

Ship Shape
and Bristol Fashion
DONALD BRABBINS and EDWARD FYFFE

Recorded on the evening of their arrest
at the Fortune Theatre, London on 2nd May, 1959

← STEREO →
Can Also Be Played in Mono

BFLP203

Ship Shape and Bristol Fashion

DONALD BRABBINS and EDWARD FYFFE

SIDE ONE

1. **KNOCKING OUT A CRAFTY ONE**
   (Brabbins-Fyffe)

2. **THERE'S A LAY-BY ON THE A13 ...**
   (Brabbins-Fyffe)

3. **THE OLD TOWN OF LESBOS**
   (Brabbins-Fyffe-Russell)

4. **THE PERINEUM SONG** *(Brabbins-Fyffe)*

5. **MRS PALMER** *(Brabbins-Fyffe)*

6. **PUCKER UP AND BLOW** *(Brabbins-Fyffe)*

SIDE TWO

1. **THE SWINGER'S LAMENT** *(Brabbins)*

2. **HAVE YOU EVER HAD TO TAKE A SHIT ON A TRAIN?** *(Brabbins-Fyffe)*

3. **JOHNNY BLOODY FOREIGNER**
   (Brabbins-Fyffe)

4. **ROHYPNOL** *(Brabbins-Fyffe)*

5. **SEEING TO THE MISSUS**
   (Brabbins-Fyffe-Russell)

6. **G. A. Y.** *(Trad. Arr. Fyffe)*

The unholy marriage between Donald Brabbins and Teddy Fyffe continues to bear fruit on the London stage, and this, their first long-player, preserves it like the finest compote. Their blithe estrangement from the prevailing winds of taste and decency is a thing of marvel, and one can only admire the fortitude with which they have endured an innumerable array of fines, cautions, prison sentences and, of course, in Teddy Fyffe's inimitable case, long-term house arrests.

Luckily, the vigour with which they have been pursued by the Crown is amply matched, and indeed exceeded, by the affection in which they are held by the British public. There can be scarcely a man, woman or child in the land that hasn't downed tools and joined them in full-throated song whenever their celebrated revue hits town; now, with the purchase of this LP, every nursery in the kingdom may similarly enjoy the simple pleasures of 'The Perineum Song', the upbeat syncopation of 'Pucker Up And Blow' featuring Larry Adler on harmonica, and the delicately wrought subtlety of Donald Brabbins' tear-jerking prose-poem 'The Swinger's Lament'.

Notes by Bertrand Russell

FIRST TRUMP

REGD. TRADEMARK OF
THE ARMSTRONG & MILLER
RADIOGRAM CO. LTD.

LONG PLAY 33⅓ R.P.M

℗1959

A Stereo Pickup of maximum 8 gr stylus force
(Maximum tip radius 0,7 mil) is recommended

GLORIOUS MAGS

Words and music by Donald Brabbins & Teddy Fyffe
Copyright © 1967 FYFFE & DRUM MUSIC INC.
Reprinted with kind permission from *'Brown Sauce'* published by The Bodley Head

1. Porn, porn, wonderful porn!
   There's nothing quite like it
      For stirring the horn
   So come let us linger
      With outstretched ... finger
   As we turn o'er the pages
      Of our mag-a-zines!

2. So many memories of titles of yore
   Fiesta, Men Only, New Talent and Score
      Escort and Rustler
      Razzle and Hustler
   A few of the mags concealed in my drawer

3. I liked it classy, tasteful and glossy
   He liked it dirty,
      More scuzzy and drossy
   I liked the stories
      They had some appeal
   And he liked the letters –
      Who cares they're not real

4. Porn, porn, wonderful porn!
   The top shelf of Menzies it used to adorn
   To buy one (it's true) was quite a fine art
   Concealed in the pages
      Of Exchange and Mart

5. Now I am old I've foregone my archive
   But there's one thing I miss
      From when 'twas alive:
   If you feared discovery
      No need to connive
   It was easy to burn them –
      Not like a hard drive

6. Porn, porn, wonderful porn!
   There's nothing quite like it
      For stirring the horn.
   So come let us linger
      With outstretched ... finger.
   As we celebrate memories
      Of glor-i-ous mags!

Clip - pe - ty   clop - pe - ty

Clip   clop   clip   clop

IN PRAISE OF BURLESQUE

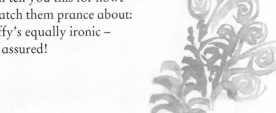

For those gentlemen who nurse a guilty penchant
Those who long to slip to Soho after hours
There's a night in town
    that needn't be your swansong
If you listen to this sage advice of ours ...

We've discovered a type of highbrow entertainment
That features feathers, naked girls, balloons, the lot
If your conscience won't abide exploited females,
    STOP!
        Is this pornographic?
                No it is not.

It's not dirty
    It's burlesque
It would be hurtful
    And grotesque
To suggest that there was something untoward
In watching women do the splits
While they liberate their bits
From lacy panty,
    diamanté
        and velour

Admittedly they strip
But it's witty
    Like a quip
An ironic take on glamour and allure

And I'll tell you this for nowt
As I watch them prance about:
My stiffy's equally ironic –
    Be assured!

Words and music by Donald Brabbins & Teddy Fyffe
Copyright © 1965 (AMI)
Alternative version recorded available on
'Tyter Later', Trump Recordings BF1045

SEEDLEIGH SCHOOL
KETTERINGHAM NR. NORWICH

Friday 14th May

Dear Dad

Thank you for the pen you sent me for my birthday. I am writing with it now. School is ok I suppose, though the rugby pitch is waterlogged so we have had to stay inside for games. Mum said I can come and stay with you at half term which would be great. Maybe we could go and see London Irish again?

Love

Paul

P.S. This might sound silly but Mark watson has been put on bin duty for interfering with himself, and Mr Creed said if he does it again he might go blind. Can that really happen?

I.T.&T.
Satellite Systems Limited

Unit 74
Albermarshe Industrial Estate
Hatfield Road
Wembley
HA9 7RQ
Tel. 0345 7788 4422
Fax. 0345 7788 4423
www.ittss-limited.biz.uk

18/05

Dear Paul,

Great to hear from you, and so pleased you like the
pen. It works with ink and with cartridge so should
see you alright. Half-term is definitely a go project
as far as I'm concerned. The Irish play Leicester
Tigers on the 12th so with a bit of luck we can both
be there to cheer them on!

Loads of love

Dad

PS:
Paul, interfering with yourself will not send
you blind, in spite of what Mr. Creed might
say. Masturbation, as all intelligent grown-ups
call it, is one of the most natural things in
the world. That is, unless you use a ligature,
like for example Michael Hutchence. Then it's
well kinky. Mind you, gasping, as they call
it, is not without its risks, so beware. If
you want to put your faith in a thin slice of
orange go ahead, but I've yet to find a fruit
that's tart enough to bring me round, which is
why your mother was always so useful.

SEEDLEIGH SCHOOL
KETTERINGHAM NR. NORWICH

Saturday night (Late!)

Dear Dad,

Half term was brilliant, thanks Dad. Looks like the Irish are now going to make it to the semis of the Heineken Cup, hope we don't have to play Toulouse again that would be a disaster. With any luck we will get Leicester Tigers instead, I reckon we'd have the edge on them.

Mum says she might come up to school for my confirmation at the end of term would you like to come? Fabrice isn't coming with her, she says they are having a bit of time apart. Maybe we could all go for tea in Ketteringham after?

Love

Paul.

P.S. Ian willets found a girly magazine in the Bluebell woods but Mr Creed confiscated it. He said it was a sin to look at pornography and any boy that had seen the magazine was going to hell is that true?

I.T.&T.
Satellite Systems Limited

Unit 74
Albermarshe Industrial Estate
Hatfield Road
Wembley
HA9 7RQ
Tel. 0345 7788 4422
Fax. 0345 7788 4423
www.ittss-limited.biz.uk

Thursday night (L8R!)

Dear Paul

Yes it was great to see you, and, yes the Tigers would be a
good draw for the semis. Imagine if we make it to the final!
Bob Cord, our marketing guy has some contacts in the
hospitality world and might be able to wangle a couple of
tickets, I'll let you know how that goes.

I'm going to try hard and make it to your confirmation
though we've got a big job on next month down in Surrey fitting
out one of the new Bannatyne sports centres so it might be
tricky making it along for tea. Either way I'll definitely be
there for the service, you can count on me!

Loads of love

Dad xxx

P.S. Paul, of course you won't go to hell if you look at
pornography. Pictures designed to stimulate sexual interest
have been around since the time of the Cerne Abbas Giant
(a large drawing of a man with an erect penis carved by
prehistoric man into the chalk hills of Dorset) and are very
much part of the cultural landscape whether people like it or
not. There are countless pornographic images in the decorative
urns of the Ancient Greeks, in the Roman mosaics of Pompeii,
and also in that battered leather suitcase with the sellotape
on the handle that I keep on top of my wardrobe. Seriously,
there are some real collectors items in there including
some great vintage BDSM, and I'm not talking that soft-soap
Betty Page nonsense, I mean the real set-your-teeth-on-edge,
glimpse-through-your-fingers eyewatering genuine article.

So no, you're not going to hell, but with that little
collection to spur you on you may, like me, find yourself
under a surgeon's care with a split frenulum and a twisted
testicle, so be warned!!! You should have seen your
mother's face when I told her she was going to have
to release me from the stirrups and drive me to casualty,
she nearly dropped the mallet!!

SEEDLEIGH SCHOOL
KETTERINGHAM NR. NORWICH

Tuesday June 8th

Dear Dad,

Thanks so much for coming last week. I felt a bit of a dobber in my suit etc. but it was great to see you and mum in the school chapel and not even arguing for a change! Really pleased that you made it along for ka. Mum told me after you left that she thought you were really looking handsome and that it was really kind of you to pay the bill.

After you left we went for a walk along the river and she told me that Fabrice has moved out of their apartment and she is thinking of moving back to England. Who knows, she might end up back in Perivale on the old estate! Wouldn't that be weird you having mum for a neighbour!? Can't believe we might be going to see the semis! Shame we drew Toulouse but you never know...

Lots of Love

Paul

P.S. Matthew Heaton says that he kissed Tilly swain in the holidays when she was still my girlfriend. Made me really upset, even though we're not going out anymore.

I.T.&T.
Satellite Systems Limited

Unit 74
Albermarshe Industrial Estate
Hatfield Road
Wembley
HA9 7RQ
Tel. 0345 7788 4422
Fax. 0345 7788 4423
www.ittss-limited.biz.uk

(TGI) Friday 11 June

Dear Paul,

Yes it was lovely to see you and your Mum last weekend.
We both thought you looked so smart and grown-up, hard to
believe that you are 15 already, the years have flown by.

Great news: Bob was as good as his word and I now have...
wait for it.........three tickets for the semifinal at the
Stade-De-France. So now you can bring one of your mates
from school. The game is on a Saturday so we can hop on
the Eurostar on Friday night and have a bit of a weekend in
Paris. I'm guessing you wont be inviting Matthew Heaton! :-)

I know it can be hard to find out that a girl you have had
feelings for has been involved with someone else, but the
thing is, Paul, human beings aren't really made to have just
one partner. Wherever you look in human society, polygamy
is really the order of the day: it's just dressed up as
"affairs" or "divorce", or "a wine and cheese party".

In fact there has always been a really active scene on the
estate, and your mother and I realised very early on that if
we were going to keep our married life fresh we should do the
loving thing and allow one another to experience different
partners. It took me a while to adjust, but by the end of our
marriage I used to watch your mother get passed around the
close like a rag doll and not even bat an eyelid!

Loads of love.........

Dad   xxxxXXX

PS Great to hear your mother might be moving back.
I'll let the neighbours know, I'm sure they'll want to
give her a very warm welcome.

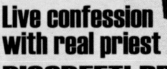

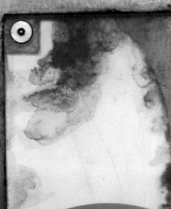

REAL TRANSUBSTANTIATION
VERY CONVINCING
SUNG EUCHARIST 7AM
FULL SERVICE 11AM
* 03378 444 219 *

FRONTISPIECE

DON'T

GET ME STARTED

OR THE

JOURNEYMAN'S GUIDE TO
PALMERSTON'S BLOODY BRITAIN.

By CHARLES DARWIN, M.A.,

FELLOW OF THE ROYAL, GEOGRAPHICAL, LINNÆAN, ETC., SOCIETIES;
AUTHOR OF 'JOURNAL OF RESEARCHES DURING H. M. S. BEAGLE'S VOYAGE
ROUND THE WORLD' AND 'ON THE ORIGIN OF SPECIES'
AND ALL-ROUND RED-BLOODED MALE.

LONDON:
DUMBRELLS, ALBEMARLE STREET.
1863.

LIST OF PLATES.

CONTENTS.

LEAFLET? LEAVE IT!

FROM NEXT YEAR, IF YOU DESIGN, PRINT, DISTRIBUTE, HANDLE OR READ UNLICENSED LEAFLETS OR FLYERS YOU WILL BE LIABLE TO PROSECUTION AND A FINE OF UP TO £10,000

In recognition of the fact that the production and distribution of leaflets is a major cause of deforestation, global warming, domestic distress, psychiatric disorders and mediocre graphic design, we are binning brochures, pulping pamphlets and liquidating leaflets. Remember, our Flyer Squad is tooled up and ready.

From January 1st, look for the new Leaflet Mark.

Don't let anything through your letterbox without it. Or go to jail.

DON'T BE A DOORMAT. DO WHAT'S RIGHT.

Alvin Stardust's sideburns were a mistake

GENERAL STUDIES ISN'T A PROPER A LEVEL

There's no future in cupcakes

WE ARE **B8** PARTNERSHIP

BRAND. NEW.

**■8 ARE BRAND DNA.
WE GENERATE.
WE INNOVATE.**

**WHAT YOU SAY
IS HOW YOU SAY IT.
WE'RE ON TOP. DOING IT.
DOING THE BUSINESS.**

**JOINED UP. THINKING.
■8 CREATE.**

**IN OUR DOMAIN,
WE ARE MASTERS.**

B8'S MASTERS:

CREATIVE: NEIL DOWNE.
Cowboy shirts, sticky-toffee pudding

STRATEGY: EMMA ROYDS.
Most notable achievement:
my collection of post-it notes

MONEY: HARDEN THICKE.
Into football, Danish butter and talking about
myself in the third person

DESIGN: IVANA MANDIC.
b. Montenegro
Likes: pistachio ice cream
Dislikes: long-haired dogs

OUR PEOPLE. YOURS.

CASE STUDY.
SPORTSFEST 2013.

London's bid for the 2013 Sportsfest was unprecedented in its scope and ambition. It proposed nothing short of a revolution. The desire to make sport reconnect with the globe's youth.

A feeling of possibility, of the future being unwritten, of our passion, our hopes, our humanity.

To make this happen, it needed a brand. A brand that could fire the collective imagination of the world, a brand that could make Sportsfest as contemporary, as relevant and as cutting edge as ever. A brand that would be a rallying cry for change.

SPORTSFEST 2013.
THE MARK.

URGENT. INVITING.
ACTIVE. FORCEFUL.
RIGHT NOW.

The emblem we created is unconventional, uncompromising, surprisingly asymmetrical. Perfectly mirroring London's status as an evolving, shifting, multi-cultural city.

At its heart is an iconic sporting image – the baton change of the relay race – emerging from a subliminal encoding of the 2013 digits.

The image reinforces the interdependence of sport, of the cooperation that is required if we are to reach our potential. And perhaps most importantly, the interconnectedness of one human generation with another.

OMIT DROP SHADOW
FOR EXECUTIONS LESS THAN 50MM IN WIDTH

MINIMUM
PERMITTED
WIDTH 18MM

PERMITTED COLOURS

THE MARK EXTENDS TO THE BOUNDS SHOWN AND INCLUDES AN AREA OF WHITE SPACE
MAINTAIN CLEAR MARGIN AROUND MARK EQUIVALENT TO AT LEAST 20% OF REPRODUCED DIMENSION

SPORTSFEST 2013.
THE PERSONALITY.

INTRODUCING COCKROFT AND WHEATLEY.
FOR THE KIDS.
(OF ALL AGES.)

The brand also needed a strong character focus, and after a great deal of consultation with youth groups and end-users, we created a powerful, malleable basis for virtual and video interactions with the birth of Cockroft and Wheatley, the Sportsfest 2013 mascots.

Already proving an unstoppable hit with old and young alike, these irrepressible designs manage to be both effortlessly contemporary and reassuringly familiar.

In all executions size is unimportant.

SPORTSFEST 2013.
THE MASTER PLAN.

360° BRAND.
BIG DREAMS.
RISING TO THE
OCCASION.

Central to the B8 realisation of the Sportsfest 2013 project has been an understanding that it is the interface between brand and user that determines experience. When that experience survives, the result is known as legacy.

The brand we created will shape the world's experience of Sportsfest 2013. Digital media will help to create an experience which exists outside the constraints of time and space, and a festival in which everyone can participate.

The brand will take Sportsfest beyond sport, into something that endures, regenerates and renews. When the Athletes' Village is long gone, brand will survive. In the digital age, brand is legacy and legacy is brand.

B8: MASTERING
BRAND OVER AND
OVER AGAIN.

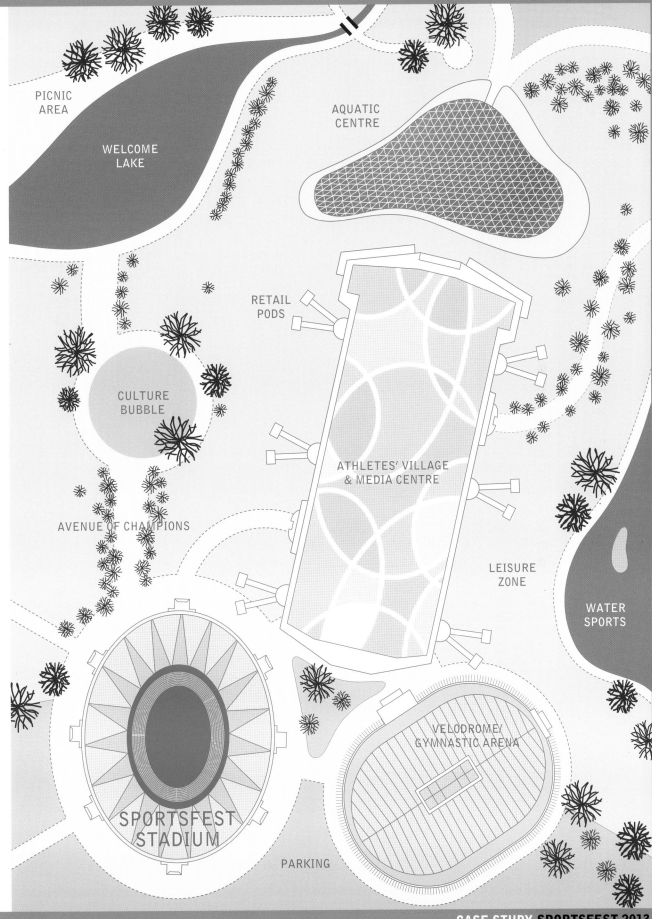

PICNIC
AREA

WELCOME
LAKE

AQUATIC
CENTRE

RETAIL
PODS

CULTURE
BUBBLE

ATHLETES' VILLAGE
& MEDIA CENTRE

AVENUE OF CHAMPIONS

LEISURE
ZONE

WATER
SPORTS

SPORTSFEST
STADIUM

VELODROME/
GYMNASTIC ARENA

PARKING

matesbook

Search 🔍

Home   Profile   Account ▾

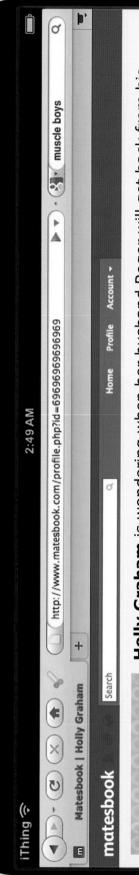

Holly Graham is wondering when her husband Roger will get back from his fact-finding mission in Torquay

Wall   Info   Photos   Events   +

What's on your mind?

Attach: 🖼 📷 ✂ 📄

▾ 🔒 ▾   **Share**

🔍 Options

View Photos of Holly (422)

View Videos of Holly (52)

Send Holly a Message

Poke Holly

Information

Married
36C-24-36

Mutual Mates

Peter

RECENT ACTIVITY

🔲 Holly joined the group He'd Get It

▦ Peter Blakey invited Holly to Tom Creech's Toga Party

👥 Holly and Russell Brand are now mates

🖊 Holly likes Peter Blakey's new photo album My new Aussiebums

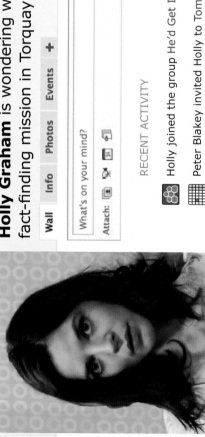

Roger Graham Darling??? Is this you???! I didn't know you had one of these pages??

Thu at 2.40am · Comment · Like

Holly Graham Roger! What are you doing here?

Thu at 2.40am · Comment · Like

Roger Graham Well it's rather a long story. I was trying to contact Peter at the office, but he's been out all afternoon. So I thought, 'I wonder if he's on that Matesbook thing?' Then I saw that he'd repeatedly poked you.

Thu at 2.41am · Comment · Like

Holly Graham Gosh, lol :-)

Peter Blakey Look weve got to stop all this cloak and dagger stuff Holly. Its time we just came right out and explained to Roger exactly whats been going on

Thu at 2.41am · Comment · Like

 Roger Graham Peter??!! Are you there too? But...?

Thu at 2.41am · Comment · Like

 Peter Blakey Hello Rog. Yes, I am. Im round at your place because ... Well I suppose theres no point in delaying the inevitable. The thing is Rog... Ive been helping Holly with your wireless internet

Thu at 2.46am · Comment · Like

 Roger Graham Oh pitysticks, is it playing up again?

Thu at 2.46am · Comment · Like

 Peter Blakey Im afraid so Rog. Its been terribly frustrrating. First we tried to get a signal in the hallway then we moved through into the lounge then halfway up the stairs until finally in coplete desperation I tried to log on in the spare bedroom. Then, what do you know? The second you come online its back up to full strength

Thu at 2.47am · Comment · Like

 Roger Graham What an irony! Tahnk goodnesss you were able to drop by. And I have to say - and this is going to sound dreadful - but it's good to know someone's keeping an eye on Holly. I'm not a jealous man, but seven weeks in Torquay starts to play tricks with a man's mind.

Thu at 2.48am · Comment · Like

 **Peter Blakey** Its the very least I could do Roger. Oh by the way - can you hang on down there just a couple more days? The background youre giving us on the Weetalumps campaign is dynamite. Ooh hang on - yes, definiteily back in business here now. Ive even got one solid bar on the desk in your study. Must dash

Thu at 2.49am · Comment · Like

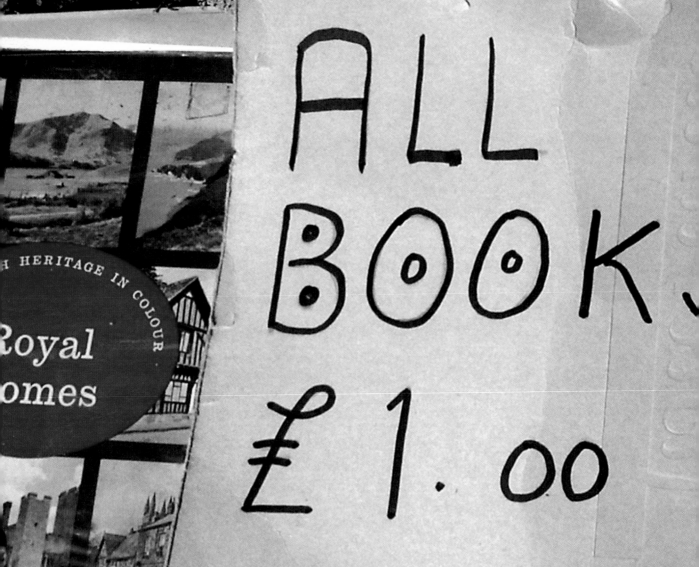

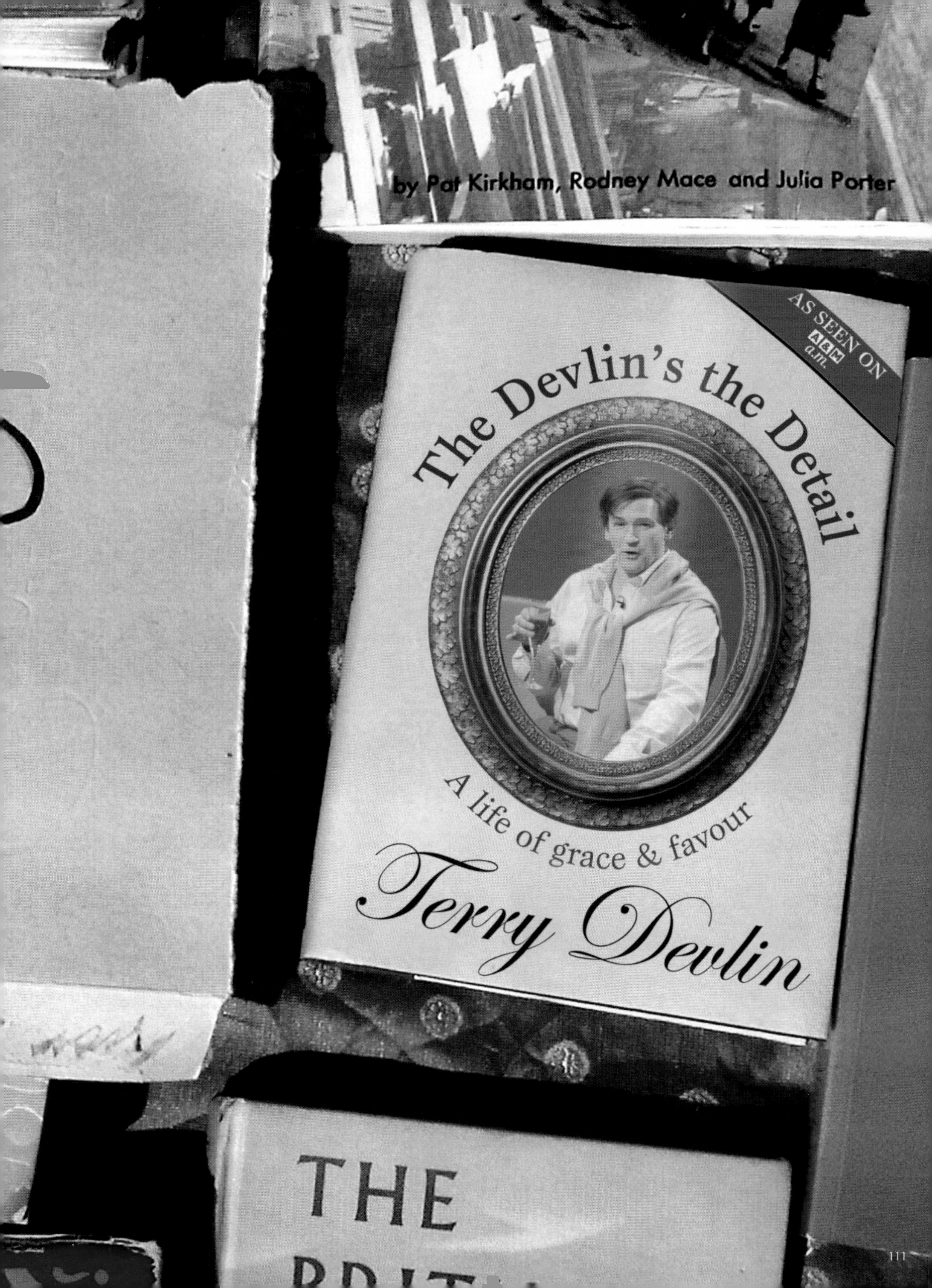

by Pat Kirkham, Rodney Mace and Julia Porter

AS SEEN ON
a.m.

The Devlin's the Detail

A life of grace & favour

Terry Devlin

THE

To Diana
princess of my heart

To the Manner Born

"Congratulations, Mrs Devlin, it's a boy!" And with that, the midwife, an English woman (typical County Down!) named Rose, passed me over to my poor, exhausted, sainted 32-year-old mother.

Maureen Boyle—even to write that poor, sainted woman's name brings a lump to my throat—had once had it all. The young beauty queen from Newtonards had married young—they all did those days—to Seamus Devlin the handsome mechanic from Ronnie's Motors. The day of their marriage, October 30th 1956, seemed to promise so, so much: mild and sunny in a way that seemed to cling to the memories of the summer just gone rather than anticipate the winter that was just around the corner. A bitter, bitter winter as it turned out. Historically bitter.

Seamus and Maureen's first two years were spent feathering their new nest in Ballymena Road, an old fashioned slum dwelling with a poky downstairs room and a smoky kitchen with an ancient range stove and two small bedrooms and a bathroom above, and a very small loft-space above that, only accessible by ladder which had to be borrowed from the MacLarrys over the road. By February 1966 they had four children: Seamus Junior, Patrick (Patty as he was to all of us, God rest his immortal soul), Angela (her father's daughter to be sure), and Kevin. By the time I arrived in 1968 the Devlin brood had outgrown the charms of that tiny house. The crisis was alleviated somewhat by the fact that Da spent the best part of day and night in Ryan's public saloon and when he came back it was to all our benefits that there wasn't the space for him to swing his fist as much as he would have liked. But they were happy days. Rough and happy.

Many years later when I was privileged enough to be covering Diana, Princess of Wales' trip to India with her husband, Charles, the Prince of Wales, I was able to look that other truly sainted and exhausted woman in the eye and say that yes, I, Terry Devlin, understood the cold place she found herself in, frozen out of the affections of her supposed husband, deserted by the family she had grown up amongst. A sacrificial lamb, a butterfly upon a wheel, a hunted beast, a pure, white hart caught in the thicket of a cruel man's indifference. (Although the Prince of Wales is now a fine upstanding king-in-waiting and his wife the fragrant Duchess of Cornwall is truly a jewel, I tell you that for nothing.)

At the age of five, the young Terry Devlin had absolutely no idea what life had in store for him. He was chasing butterflies. The Troubles were four years old by then and my memories of our time in Ardrossan Close—the house to which we moved from Ballymena Road in 1970; three bedrooms, new-build, small garden, utility room, loft, built-in ladder, pebbledash—are of convoy after convoy of army 4-tonners filled with cheery squaddies with jaunty plumes in their berets. Ours was a solidly loyalist household so it was felt that the presence of Her Majesty's forces was surely a good thing, although in truth it seemed to merely stoke the flames of the republicans.

In 1974 Ryan's public saloon was fire-bombed so Da had to find somewhere else to spend his days. He had become involved in the Ulster Vanguard and was spending a great deal of his time discussing 'the battlelines' with his drinking friends. Robert Campbell—who years later confessed to being involved in the bombing of the Tramore Bar for which the Ryan's bombing had been revenge—was often around Ardrossan Close. Everyone was sore about the provos bombing on the mainland—there had been several London bombings in the Winter. The Assembly tried to get itself going but Ian Paisley led a rowdy protest that Da joined in with.

However, the Queen was awfully busy. She had dazzled everyone at the opening of London's new bridge, London Bridge, earlier in the year. Her dependable Hardy Amies

I'll never forget the moment that Lady Di looked down from the balcony on her wedding day, saw me and said, 'Terry you are my ROCK! Promise me you will never leave my side.'

I've always had a very very special bond with the Princess Royal. She understands me better than anyone since me mam. In another life we were brothers.

Shy Di in salmon pink waving that same hand that moments before had playfully slapped mine. 'Of course I'll come back Terry, you Silly!'

Oh, they were cruel to this poor poor woman. Look: they even made her stand next to Fergie.

look was bedding in beautifully now. The pale blues that her mother Queen Elizabeth the Queen Mother carried so well framed the dark-haired monarch and mother of four so well.

Later that year of course Princess Anne was very much to marry Captain Mark Phillips in a terribly moving service at Westminster Abbey. Her young brother Edward—only nine years of age—was, as it were, 'page-boy' at the ceremony. Princess Anne wore a plain 'Tudor-style' wedding dress with a high collar and medieval sleeves while the dashing young captain who had stolen her royal heart was done up to the very nines in the finery of his regiment: scarlet, blue and dazzling gold as befitting a young man serving at the rank of Captain in the Queen's Dragoon Guards. Lady Sarah Armstrong-Jones (later to become Lady Sarah Chatto), daughter of Princess Margaret and first cousin to the Princess, and also nine years old, was 'bridesmaid' for the wedding.

So the first of Her Royal Majesty's offspring was hitched. Would it last? What would the omens be for this noble family? Might it possibly be that her children would all marry happily and provide stability for their families and for the nation? Might the sainted Lady Diana Spencer, only 12 years old at this point, have been one of the estimated 500 million people who watched the dazzling ceremony on television? And if she did, might she have uttered up a little prayer that she would one day be a princess? What might she have fancied her life to be as a royal fairytale princess? Might she ever in her wildest dreams have imagined that her destiny was being designed right there that day? Had she even heard of the Pont de L'Alma? Had she heard of Paris? What did she know of the white Fiat Uno, at that stage not even built, that was to decide her fate?

Praise for
The Devlin's the Detail

'Terry Devlin brings a royal perspective to his
heart-rending story as we move from province to palace at a
white-knuckle gallop. After years of deafening silence here,
at last, is a book about The Princess of Wales'
Lorraine Kelly, GMTV

'Mr. Devlin's having been a "royal correspondent"
is all very well'
Rod Liddle, *The Spectator*

'Terry Devlin ... knowing ... the Princess ... [of] ...
Wales ... unlike *any* other'
Simon Jenkins, *Sunday Telegraph*

'This book raises all kinds of questions about royal access
and, indeed, protocol'
Sir Robert Janvrin

From the same author:
The Crumbs From Under Thy Table
Backstairs, Backstabs & Backsides
Terry Devlin's Right Royal Sudokus

ISBN 0-330-41926

90100

9 783330 419262

Laughter *(can enhance well-being)*

You're severely obese, madam. I suggest for your
own health you consider losing some weight.

Abide with me, 'tis eventide! The day is past and gone;
The shadows of the evening fall; the night is coming on.

I'm sorry I'm late. I overslept.

M'dekk to mothership. There's a human child in
here with a cooking utensil stuck on his head.
Is there anything we can do to help?

A. AAA. AAAAA. AAAAAA.
I am actually struggling to make out the last line.

Tweet tweet tweet. Tweet tweet.

LISA'S LOOKS

Flushed with the success of her upmarket adult boutique Boudoir d'Amour, Lisa Varey went viral when a webcam buddy persuaded her to share her makeup tips on video-sharing website YourBox. Her 'No Trowel Required' tutorials notched up 'literally dozens' of hits and now she's slapping a monthly dose of sassy style all over our pages.

#1
Rihanna Rude Boy Look

My husband didn't recognise me when I sashayed into the lounge in a split-leg dark blue cocktail dress wearing this Rihanna-style make-up. Mind you, he hadn't been home for a week, I'm surprised he even remembered the number of the house.

#2
Second Date Tease Look

Give the contestant a glimpse of what he could have won with this catch-me-if-you-can, woman-of-mystery, absolutely-no-chance-of-put-in look.

#3
Sexy Slave Girl Look

Imagine you are a native girl at the whim of a domineering master with this fresh, contemporary make-up. Or try working the late shift at the cash-and-carry on Heatley Green – it's much the same thing.

#4
Frisky Milkshake Look

Bring your man's temperature to a rolling boil with this saucy look designed to titillate and provoke. Please note, do not attempt if you have a slight 'tache as the combined influence of jawline shades will make you look like Brian Blessed in 'Henry V'.

#5
Girl At The Top Look

This high-powered work make-up will make you the Queen of the boardroom. Combine with a trouser suit or go the whole hog with a city pinstripe. Why should dykes have all the fun?

#6
You Told Me That Before Look

While Hubby drones on about his plans for the compost heap, let your smoky eyeliner and highlight brush do the work with this uncontrollable-urge-to-yawn look. Seriously though, they do like to talk about themselves, don't they girls? Anyone would think we were listening.

#7
Faulty Drain Look

They say that Orpheus glanced at Eurydice, thus commiting her soul to Hades. Well you can have something of the same effect with this withering eye make-up. Perfect for Tesco home delivery men, single mothers from the estate, and that man who works the barrier at the multistorey in Westgate.

#8
Angel Fairy Eyes Look

It's every little girl's dream to meet Prince Charming and ride off into the sunset. Make your wishes come true with this romantic make-up designed to bring out the hero in your fella. At the same time, be realistic. Even George Clooney shakes it off on to the pedestal rug.

#9
Leona Bleeding Heart Look

Leona Lewis burst onto the scene from nowhere when she got noticed by Simon Cowell and a whole nation took her to their hearts. That sort of thing will never happen to you. Still, you can give yourself the same make-up, which is something I suppose.

#10
Vintage Glam Look

Move over Marc Bolan! Not too far on to the verge though, there's a tree coming up! Whoops!!!

#11
Sultry Blues Look

Just now and then we all need to let ourselves off the leash and behave like a common tramp. That's in the American sense of the word, of course. I'm not suggesting you score a six pack of Thunderbird and start shouting at traffic.

#12
Colour Explosion Look

Men have it so easy, don't they? I bought two new blender brushes (not cheap), two new primers, and worked for three nights on the trot perfecting this make-up so I'd look like a million dollars on my man's arm for his fortieth birthday. I count myself lucky if he washes his balls once a week.

#13
Icy Peacock Look

Tesco don't put everything they've got on the shelves, so why should you? Leave a little to the imagination with this super sophisticated make-up with just a hint of Jane Lynch from 'Glee'. Not that you've got shoulders like hers! Honestly, she's a handsome woman but she looks like she works on the roads.

#14
Babe In Arms Look

A look that leaves you as innocent as the day you were born, like a swaddled nymph washed up on the shores of Elysium. How are they to know you aren't wearing any knickers?!

Welcome! Sign in or let us harvest your data.

Go

My eTat | Buy tat | Get rid of tat | Con

CATEGORIES ▼ | GENERAL TAT | REAL OLD SHIT | FOUND IN A BUS SHELTER | DAILY DEAL

Watch this bit of tat

Night of The Never Endin
(1988 Paperback)
HORROR

----SHIPPING DISCOUNTS OFFERED----08

Item condition:	**Quite tatty**
Time left:	**43m 10secs** (Jun 28, 2
Bid history:	0 bids

Starting bid:	**UK £0.25**
Your max bid:	**UK £**
	(Enter UK £0.25 or more)

Shipping:	**£2.99** Royal Mail Seco
	Estimated delivery within 21-2
Returns:	Buyer pays return shipp

🔒**eTat Buyer Protection** **NEW! learn n**
Not available for this real old t

Seller info
MastahJoshi14 (3) 👽
0% Positive Feedback

Ask a question
Save this seller
See other old tat from this seller
See this seller's Tat Store

Other item info

Item number:	170491664581
Item location:	East Dulwich, London
Ships to:	Worldwide
Payments:	**CrudPay** See details

Description	**Shipping and Payments**

Seller assumes all responsibility for this listing.
Item specifics - Fiction & Literature Books

Condition:	Tatty. A book that has been read but in reasonable general condition. Some rubbing to cover, adhesions to various pages... Read more
Format:	Paperback

Sydney Peabody made his way carefully to his pigeon coop. It was his pride and joy but there was a cruel wind in the air. It had been blowing ever since news of the so-called melt-faced virus had broken.

Sydney had read in his tabloid only that morning that the virus was supposed to have come off of a crashed space satellite and it was causing people and animals to go mad with violence and then make their faces melt off.

'Load of rubbish,' thought Sydney. 'I don't care about any of that science stuff anyway. I'm a working man and I care about things I know about. Like my pigeons.' He had been keeping pigeons for nigh-on twenty years and they were the only things he loved in his life – even including Doris, his put-upon wife.

'I'm coming, my darlings,' Sydney called out as he put his hand on the door of the rickety old coop. There was quite a commotion emerging from inside – a cacophony of billing and cooing. For a moment Sydney wondered if a fox had got in.

'Errol,' he called out. Errol was his favourite bird – loyal and clever and as sharp as a knife. Sydney opened the door. But nothing could have prepared him for the sight that greeted him, like a vision from the jaws of Hell itself.

Facing him were thirty rows of black beady eyes – fierce with hatred and violence. They were like his pigeons but it was as if they were now monsters. Their feathers had melted into a sickly grey gloop – but their little beaks were still as sharp as razor blades.

They launched themselves at Sydney, their coos like demon's cries.

'No,' shouted Sydney. 'Not my loves. Not my darlings.'

But they were the last words he would ever speak. Three of the birds clutched his lips in their curled claws and another of them, the cleverest and biggest, Errol himself, reached into Sydney's mouth and pecked out his vocal chords. Blood plumed like a drinking fountain and Sydney gargled it in agony. And then the rest of the birds were upon him gathering around his crotch. And they began to feast.

* * * * *

Bernie Redding's hand trembled as it rested on the handle of Olive Richard's bedroom door. He opened it and slipped expectantly inside.

'Bernie!' Olive's whisper allayed his fears.

She was lying nude as nature intended on the top of her sheets. It was, after all, a warm night. The full moon that shone through the open curtains was sufficient for Bernie to see every curve of her woman's body.

Her ladybusts were perfectly rounded like Edam cheeses and just as firm – the twin points risen and pink like mice's noses. Her thighs were parted and almost guiltily she snatched her searching fingers away from them.

'Oh, Bernie, I was thinking about you,' she sighed as he seated himself on the edge of the purple velour bedspread. 'It was so horrible today – seeing Cliff's face melt off like that.'

She sobbed and he reached out to her, holding her tightly. Slim fingers rummaged at the front of his jeans, perhaps to determine the purpose of his visit, and Olive laughed softly as she felt his rock hard man-ness therein.

Bernie began to take off his clothes until he was stood there before her as Adam had once stood before Eve – tempting her to tempt him. Her fingers closed around his sextube and squeezed like a milkmaid milking a cow. Then she pulled herself on to him.

'I was beginning to think you didn't like me.'

He thrust into her damp warm cave of pleasure like a piledriver – unable to hold back any longer.

'Does that answer your worries?' he sighed.

But her answer was lost in a medley of moans and writhings as they reached the ultimate possible peak of pleasure which any man and woman can climb.

Afterwards they lay together having a cuddle. Eventually Olive spoke.

'Oh Bernie,' she said, 'I hope you used a johnnie.'

New from **Sean M. Shitt**, high priest of incessant, relentless, never-ending, endless horror ...

Night of the Never Ending Nightmare

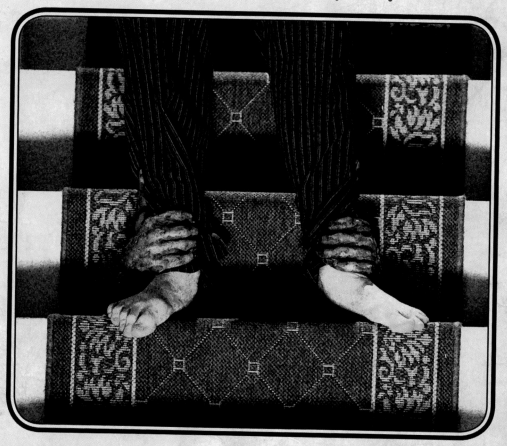

In an exclusive private school students sexually assault and mutilate their teachers and then their faces melt off.

At a seaside resort hundreds of lesbians gathering for a political conference sexually assault and mutilate each other. Then their faces melt off.

Somewhere off the Cornish coast ten thousand giant mutated lobsters with melting faces are massing, their clacking pincers harbingers of death, mutilation and sexual assault.

Or is it all a dream?
Or should that be a nightmare?
A never-ending nightmare.
That never ends.

A+M
NEW HORROR LIBRARY

#2806

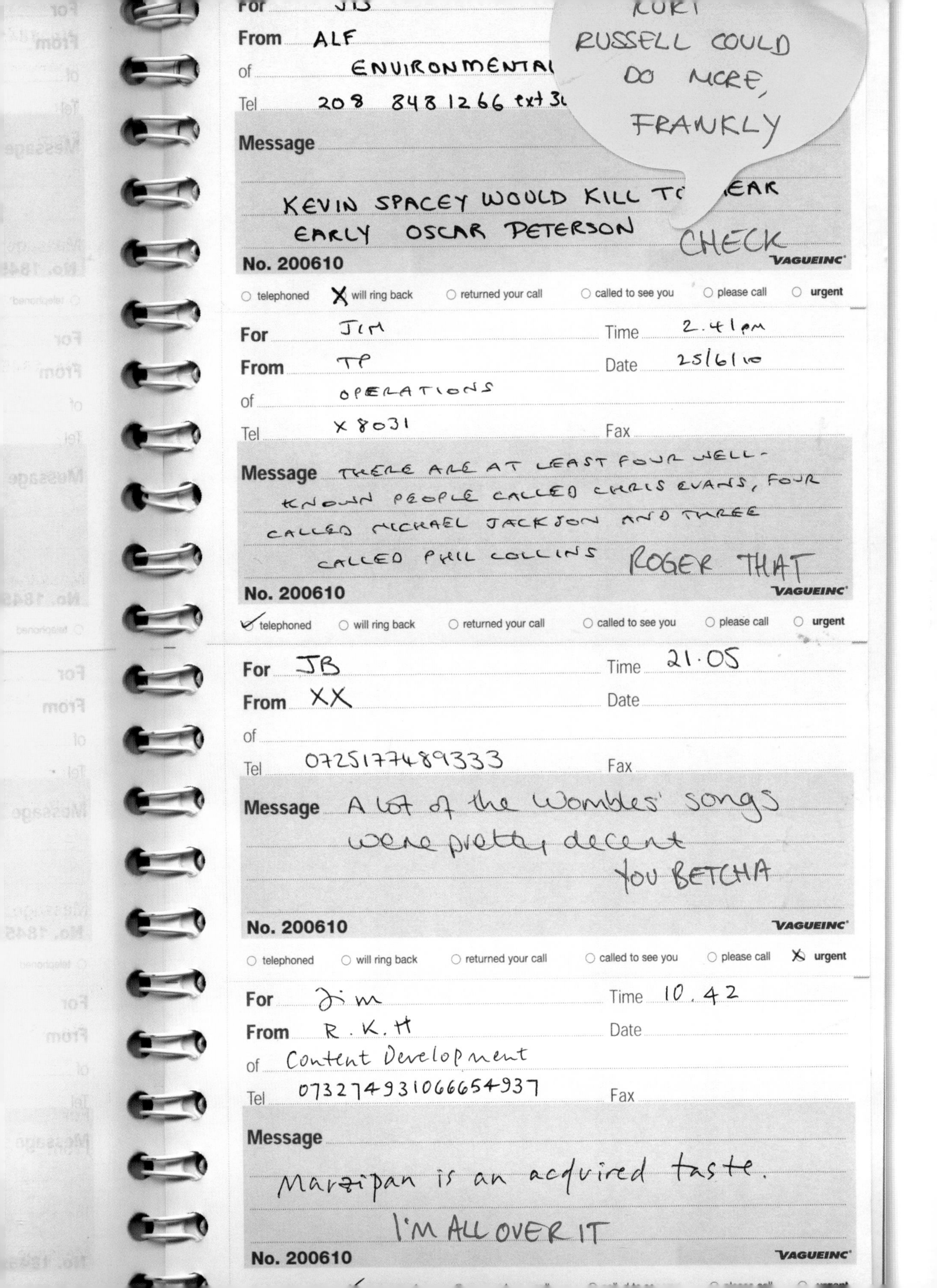

For **JB**
From **ALF**
of **ENVIRONMENTAL**
Tel **208 848 1266 ext 3...**

Message

KEVIN SPACEY WOULD KILL TO HEAR EARLY OSCAR PETERSON

CHECK

(speech bubble) KURT RUSSELL COULD DO MORE, FRANKLY

No. 200610 — VAGUEINC

○ telephoned ✗ will ring back ○ returned your call ○ called to see you ○ please call ○ urgent

---

For **JIM** — Time **2.41 pm**
From **TP** — Date **25/6/10**
of **OPERATIONS**
Tel **X 8031** — Fax

Message THERE ARE AT LEAST FOUR WELL-KNOWN PEOPLE CALLED CHRIS EVANS, FOUR CALLED MICHAEL JACKSON AND THREE CALLED PHIL COLLINS

ROGER THAT

No. 200610 — VAGUEINC

✓ telephoned ○ will ring back ○ returned your call ○ called to see you ○ please call ○ urgent

---

For **JB** — Time **21.05**
From **XX** — Date
of
Tel **07251774489333** — Fax

Message A lot of the Wombles' songs were pretty decent

YOU BETCHA

No. 200610 — VAGUEINC

○ telephoned ○ will ring back ○ returned your call ○ called to see you ○ please call ✗ urgent

---

For **Jim** — Time **10.42**
From **R.K.H** — Date
of **Content Development**
Tel **0732749310666654937** — Fax

Message

Marzipan is an acquired taste.

I'M ALL OVER IT

No. 200610 — VAGUEINC

BISTROT
ARMSTRONG｜MILLER

SMALL PLATES

tirade of gammon on a colcannon network   £15
with spring onion reception
against an olive and caper deadline

angry john dory in a caramel vest   £18
with samphire dandruff
and a calvados problem

kidneys 'bristol' with lemon bruising   £14
and gay hair

a choir of sardines up on a sprout charge   £38
(for three to share)

mutton drive-by in a forced rhubarb   £16
and broad bean mélange
with unforeseen potatoes

ENTRÉES

rump 'peter mandelson' three ways,   £28
aubergine and capon benefits,
celeriac tears

beef children in a pastry bus   £21
with on-board vegetables
and a sweet potato bastard

uncle veal bound by a béchamel order   £19
after autumn fruit dealings
with dirty jabugo
(45 minute wait)

sweetbreads protest under lady's finger,   £18
cardamom mealie-meal
with a threat of nut-gumbo

saucy monkfish in a chervil bikini   £20
with unkempt spinach spill-out,
tomato nail-varnish and a squid-ink tattoo

pork dry-stone wall   £16
with apple lichen, vanilla barbed-wire,
potato sheep and a bacon and sprout tractor

20% discretionary service charge will be added to your bill

Let's Get Layed
WE TAKE ON ALL COMERS
CALL
090999
121333
YOUNG*OLD*MEN*WOMEN
JOIN IN THE ACTION
UK Baptist Lay Preachers' Association

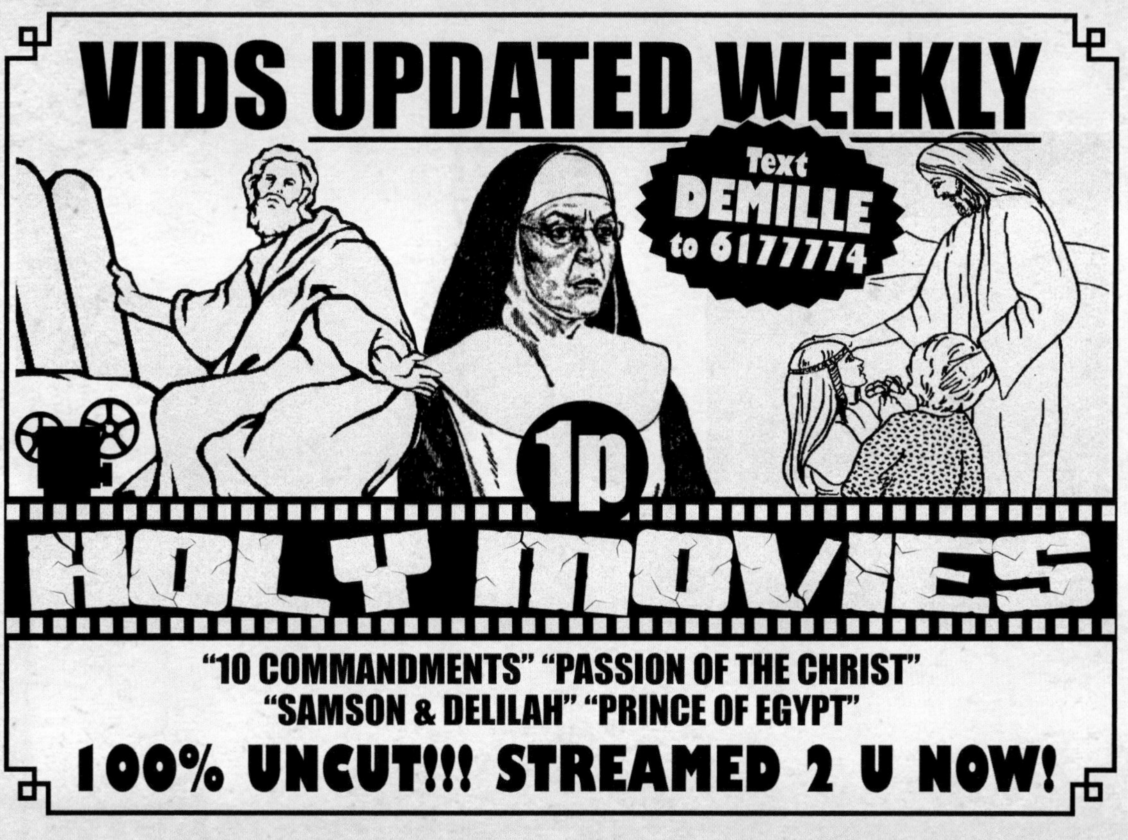
VIDS UPDATED WEEKLY
Text
DEMILLE
to 6177774
1p
HOLY MOVIES
"10 COMMANDMENTS" "PASSION OF THE CHRIST"
"SAMSON & DELILAH" "PRINCE OF EGYPT"
100% UNCUT!!! STREAMED 2 U NOW!

For: Jim Time: 10:45
From: R.K.H.
of: Content Development
Tel: 07327493106665549378 Fax:

Message: Trip switches are far too sensitive these days.

No. 200610 SAW IT COMING VAGUEINC

○ telephoned ○ will ring back ○ returned your call ○ called to see you ☑ please call ○ urgent

---

For: JB Time: 8:23 an
From: Shirley
of:
Tel: 8928 Fax:

Message: You'll never get a squirrel into trousers.

No. 200610 ARSES VAGUEINC

○ telephoned ○ will ring back ○ returned your call ○ called to see you ☑ please call ○ urgent

---

For: Mr Ballantyne Time: 05:45
From: Deborah
of:
Tel: X224 Fax:

Message: Britain's Got Talent has gone off the boil a bit. ACROSS IT

No. 200610

☑ telephoned ○ will ring back ○ returned your call ○ called to see you ○ please call

---

For: Jim Time: 10:00
From: Ellie Date: 14/02
of: HR
Tel: 09126439222483SS Fax:

Message: Everyone still likes Kevin McCloud. YOU'RE FIRED

No. 200610 VAGUEINC

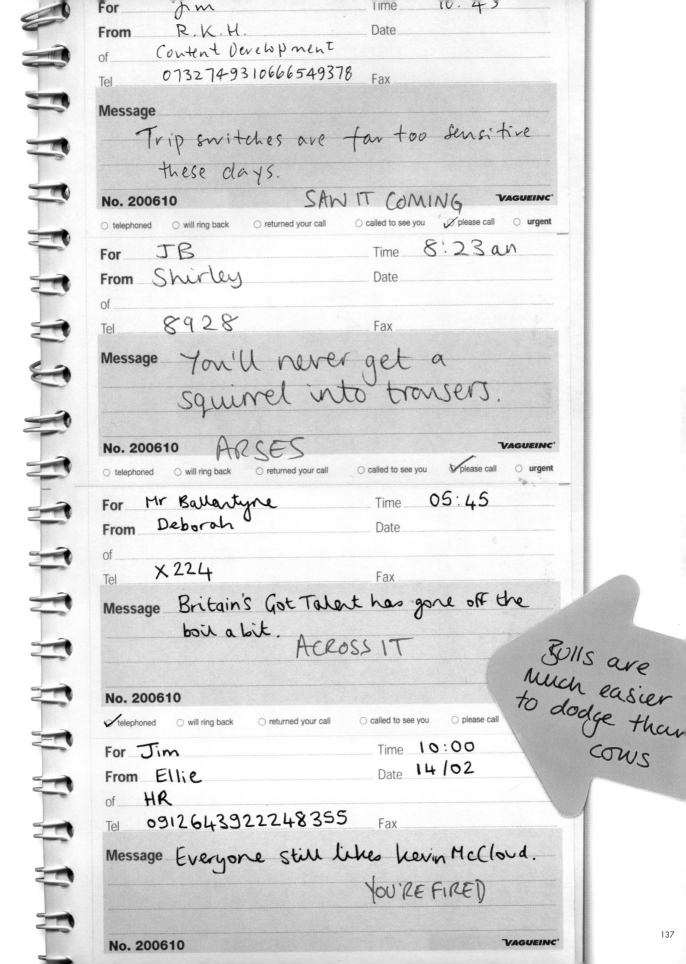

Bulls are much easier to dodge than cows

137

into the room with the silent deftness of a tiny wave scampering up a beach. Before my slumbering noggin had even that slightest presence of mind to digest his benign presence and whisk it into whatever dreamy syllabub it was wading through, he had opened the curtains, laid down the breakfast tray and unfolded the morning paper on the counterpane.

Whatever they were that the man says in the hymn 'fly forgotten as a dream dies at the tum tum day' – well, that's exactly how it was for me. Gone was the grim prospect of marriage to Lady Bertha, gone was my candidacy in the Netherton-by-Popplewell by-election and, best of all, gone was my ghastly summer-long obligation to my Aunt Augusta. This was like awakening to a kind of Valhalla – only without the burning boat, you understand.

'I trust you slept well, sir,' sang the voice I know so well.

'Indeed, indeed,' I returned, sticking a prospecting silver knife into the most perfect scroll of butter. 'In fact I've seldom slept better. You have triumphed, Veal. Even by your own high standards, this is the pip of them all.'

'Always glad to oblige, sir,' said the old Merlin, modestly scratching off the dried blood that I noticed caked around his fingernails and spattered up his starched shirt. 'And perhaps if I might be allowed to claim my recompense ...?' He produced, with a flourish, a small bowl and a razor.

'I'm not sure I understand what the deuce you're talking about,' I cautioned.

'Ahem, the small matter of your ...' he blushed and cleared his throat. 'Your moustache, sir,' he concluded.

'What of it?' I asked.

'You gave me to understand that were I to be successful in this matter, then you would allow me to shave it off.'

'I gave you no such thing,' I yelled. 'The bally cheek of it! To think that you, a shitty little servant, thought you could have dominion over anything to do with my appearance!'

And with that I leapt from the bed, caring not a jot about my state of undress, nor indeed the shameful semi-erection that had refused to leave at its appointed hour, seized the impertinent minion's bowl and proceeded to bash his sorry head in.

5

STAFFORD TAKES A TRIP

ONE THING I NEVER QUITE UNDERSTOOD about the parable of the Vineyard and Heavies, or whatever it's called, is why the blessed vineyard owner didn't just have the bally lot of them dragged away and released into the wild or whatever they did in those days.

As I remember it, he took on a bunch of ne'er-do-wells at the top of the day for an agreed price. Later that same day he took on another bunch for the same price the previous lot had accepted but for half the work. Fair enough, I say, whatever gets 'em into the vineyard. Needless to say, the working man being the same from generation e'en unto generation, the first lot get wind of the better deal the latter bunch have struck and all hell breaks loose before you can say 'shop steward'. The moral seems to be this: tough tits! Some people are better off than others and there's no point going around moaning about it.

Well this was the thought that was buzzing through the old cerebellum when I happened to bump into my cousin Archie. Archie is an interesting enough cove when all is said and done, but on this occasion he had made himself particularly eye-catching by draping a perfectly exquisite female over his arm.

'What ho, Archie,' I beamed with full cousinly *j. de v.*

'Oh,' he replied moonily, 'hullo Torquil. Have you met my *fiancée*, Rosie?' Rosie was evidently the goddess on his flank and no, I had not met her.

Here was I – the new-recruited worker joining the ranks at lunchtime – while there was Archie, a-toil in the vineyard since before breakfast. Rosie in this instance, you understand, is the vineyard. And Providence, that wise old vineyard owner. As I read it, the Bible would be very much on my side and as the parablist himself seems to be saying: 'tough tits, Archie.'

FLINT'S
Suppers
Snail Fricassée
The French call them 'escargots'...
...and snails are also known as 'chicken of the woods'!
...but they're reet slimy so we've used 100% organic chicken goujons. Sorted!
MICROWAVEABLE IN 7 MINS
Just good food. Nowt

iPod Genius throws up a few surprises
No one's allergic to peass
Fish fingers are always a good idea.
SIMON CALDECOTT'S DAD WAS TRIALLED FOR WEST HAM
What happened
Hampered by a recurring knee injury

Dalston

A Georgian gem in the heart of London's fashionable 'Badlands'

Main house: reception hall, drawing room, study, kitchen & dining room, sitting room, library, utility & cloakroom. It's way out of your league. 5 bedrooms, 4 en-suite bathrooms, family bathroom & galleried landing. Yeah, you might be kept up by gunfire every night but it's got a fucking galleried landing. Go on, fuck off. Coach House: living room, kitchen, 2 bedrooms, bathroom. Coach House. Off you fuck. Oak-framed Barn: studio, garage, workshop, wood stores. Lawned and wooded grounds extending to 4.6 acres. See? Not really the 'bang' you thought your little 'buck' might get 'out east', is it? Perhaps they'd let you lodge in the barn.

Offers invited in the region of **£ Fuck Right Off**

360° virtual tour of the house and gardens that carries more viruses than a Somali pirate on shore leave. That ought to teach you to go poking around where you have no business.

Batts Monachorum office: **jacqui.thurston@fuckoffresidential.com**   Country Department: **john.young@fuckoffresidential.com**

fuckoffresidential.com

Coming up next

David Dimbleby's Tea Shops of Britain

Gardeners' Question Time

I'm Thirteen and My Tits are Already Massive

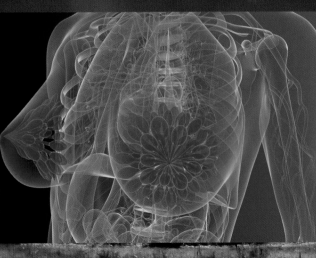

First episode of new Sunday night series in which David Dimbleby CBE traverses the length and breadth of the UK in a Land Rover and occasionally a helicopter, sampling tea, cakes and a variety of craft breads in numerous picturesque locations.

New panel-led discussion programme in which leading political figures field horticultural queries and offer advice.
This week David Willetts talks about cultivating hostas and Lord Falconer answers a difficult question about dealing with squirrels.

Powerful documentary series which looks at the psychological, social and spiritual difficulties of being in your early teens but already having massive tits.

Coming up next

A&M MAX

Do Us a Favour and Piss On that Jap

Moving drama based on the life of Bernard Manning – from his early beginning on *The Comedians* to the burning down of the Embassy Club and the death of his beloved mother. Starring Michael Sheen as Bernard Manning with Noel Clarke as Charlie Williams and James Nesbitt as Frank Carson.

64 Gay Lane

Little Zoe lives with her two dads – Glynn and Phil. But at night she has adventures with her magic torch and Esther and Rosa, the teachers who share a house next door.

Madonna della Mascardo

CAPELLA DI SANTA MARIA
PALLUZZA,
MODENA, ITALY

c. 1527 AD

The icon is now, as our photograph shows, sadly bereft of some of its once exquisitely delicate moulding, said to have been the finest vernacular carving of mediæval Europe. Though the Madonna's spirit still hovers around the ancient eaves of this humble chapel, the loss to future generations of this priceless artefact is, sadly, immeasurable. Fortunately for me I was privileged to be one of the last visitors to see the carving in its original condition. Or – to be precise – the last.

Of all the religious iconography of the sixteenth century, the Madonna della Mascardo is perhaps the most modest but also perhaps the most remarkable – a relic of an extraordinary act of faith and courage which (until recently) had survived violence, turbulence and apocalyptic upheaval.

As the Protestant forces swept southwards through Europe in 1527, on their way to the Sack of Rome, they stopped at every church and chapel, smashing any statue, any picture, any icon they could. In Paluzza they even destroyed the sacred vineyards – the source of the town's renowned Communion wine. Unbowed, unwilling to have their worship interrupted, the villagers carved their own Madonna from the trunk of an axed vine and the light of Catholic worship continued in the darkest hour of the Reformation.

Because their community was isolated in a mountainous region there was no wine to hand with which to celebrate the Eucharist. So the locals brewed their own libation – from redcurrants, nettles and dandelion leaves. Who would have believed that this concoction could be so unpalatable? Or indeed so flammable?

'The Little Prayer'

MUSEUM OF THE
CATHEDRAL OF ST OLEG
IRKUTSK, SIBERIA

c. 1680 AD

Hidden in the belfry, high above the baroque extravagance of the Ortho-
dox cathedral below, this delicate, quite beautiful, yet little-known treasure
trumps all beneath it.

Candlesticks the size of a child's fingers; a sacrament dish barely larger
than a 10 rouble piece; a finely chased, thimble-sized chalice delightfully
engraved with representations of regionally grown fruits and legumes.

The identity of the unknown smith who fashioned this miniature altar
set – known locally as 'The Little Prayer' – will never be known, but until
very recently visitors to Irkutsk could delight in its diminutive perfection.

Crafted from the finest Russian gold, beaten almost dangerously thin, the
value of these objects is – or was – absolutely incalculable. Who would have
thought that they had the fragility of antediluvian eggshells?

Not me.

It might have been thought the weight of such a venerable bell, falling so unexpectedly from a not-inconsiderable height, would have destroyed forever the fine details imparted by the goldsmith's hand. Happily, however, this was not entirely the case.

The Meggid'ah Tapestry

BUKHARA
CENTRAL ASIA

c. 974 AD

The Meggid'ah tapestry was woven during the Buwah'id dynasty and survived for over 1,000 years – or very nearly – maintained in near darkness in
order to preserve its limpid colours and frail substance.

A textile such as this was made to be given to a caliph as a gift and
created using only the finest, most priceless materials.

In fact, if you look at the photograph above – where the detail is still
visible – you will see the outline of what is, in fact, a pair of two-humped
Bactrian camels. These were delineated with a tougher, rush-based yarn
woven amongst the silk, as is attested by the fact that these are some of the
only fibres remaining in the photograph on the right.

For fragile relics such as this, the future can never be certain. It is hardly to be credited, however, that the simple incandescent electric light from the flash unit of my ordinary digital camera would prove as harmful as the most corrosive acid to fibres that have heretofore survived for centuries.

The 'Angel-glass' of Cluj

MUZEUL ETNOGRAFIC AL TRANSILVANIEI
CLUJ NAPOCA, ROMANIA

c. 1450 AD

Fashioned by the craftsmen of Cluj in the fifteenth Century, the famous Cluj vessels are some of the most beautiful objects in the world. The glassblowers of Cluj developed independently from their brethren in Venice and devised their own methods, whose secrets are guarded jealously to this day.

. The particular formula – which was rumoured to involve mixing ground silver with white sand before firing – created glassware so pure that it refracted light in such a way as to create a rainbow within its own transparency. It is so delicate that if one holds it in the air it resonates, causing it to 'sing like an angel'. Hence it is known as 'angel-glass'.

Only seven pieces are left in existence. We were lucky enough to be allowed to hold them in our own hands – an experience now to be denied to future generations.

Enlightenment

Professor Dennis Lincoln-Park is one of the world's foremost experts in art history and anthropology.

He received a KCB in 1982, a CBE in 1997 and a restraining order from the Victoria & Albert Museum in 2002.

'A beautifully illustrated record of some appalling acts of wanton destruction'
DR STEPHAN SHAMESH
Curator of The Wallace Collection

'Dennis Lincoln-Park is the master of elegant description – and the quick getaway'
WAYNE GLEAD
President of The Smithsonian Institution

'God help us – get him out of here'
CHARLES SAATCHI

HISTORY

RRP £35

ISBN 978-1-45367-222-5

A&M Global

AA Gill's voice doesn't match his photograph

KOHLRABI IS UNDERRATED FOR SALADS

No one's free on Wednesday nights

Wayne Bridge was impressed by Russell Crowe's Robin Hood

Introducing **your** library service

Department of Culture, Tourism, Sport and Prostitutes

Welcome! to your local library

We can offer you ...

Books: great short books for people new to reading, for reference or to borrow for free
Computers: free access to computers and the internet (get a login card from the front desk)
Staff to help you find what you need
Help with local and family history research
Prostitutes to satisfy your carnal desires

Families

Families are welcome in libraries. We have picture books and children's books which your children can borrow. Many libraries have story times and activities for parents and children.

Computers

We have computers in all our libraries where you can access the Internet for information.

Massage

We offer discreet and unhurried stress-relief. Our girls are adept and keen to please and can provide a full range of services including Full-Body and BBB to completion.

DATE	PROSTITUTE NAME
JAN 4 2005	Alexis
FEB 2 3 2005	Jo-Jo
APR 2 6 2005	Sindii
JUL 1 8 2006	Emma

We have

- Local studies resources where you can find out about local or family history
- Book Groups to join and sets of books for groups to use
- Newspapers and magazines to read and borrow
- Tissues, condoms, stimulants, blue pills and poppers

This month we are recommending...

Fiction

'Jane Eyre'

Charlotte Brontë's chilling gothic classic will keep you turning the pages.

Non-fiction

'Pulling Myself Together'

Denise Welch's moving autobiography reveals all about her battle with alcohol and depression.

Prostitute

'Cherry'

Naughty, kinky, adventurous, new-in-town Cherry is a very experienced lady who definitely knows how to please. Educated to A-level.

Using **your** library card

You can use your library card to borrow up to 12 items at a time, including audiobooks and DVDs. Or 2 prostitutes.

If you bring items back late we will charge a small fee.
If you bring prostitutes back late you will have to see Errol.

Fuck Off Associates
PRESTIGE PROPERTIES

Bijou Studio in the Heart of Belgravia
Canesten Mews · SW1

Detached 1 bed chalet-style single-storey studio house. Great potential for remodelling (subject to PP). Private garage. Footpath access to subway and Hyde Park Corner and world-famous shops of Park Lane. Available for first time in some 50 years. Set within the Grosvenor conservation area.

About 24 sq. ft.

Offers invited in excess of
£ Eye-wateringly Expensive

28 months' lease remaining. Now fuck off.

MAYFAIR j.cunliffe@fuckoffassociates.com   KENSINGTON a.cronan@fuckoffassociates.com

Free with **the custodian** Thursday 11.06.09

Brabbins & Fyffe
at Dovecote:
a legend in the making
BY PENELOPE FYFFE

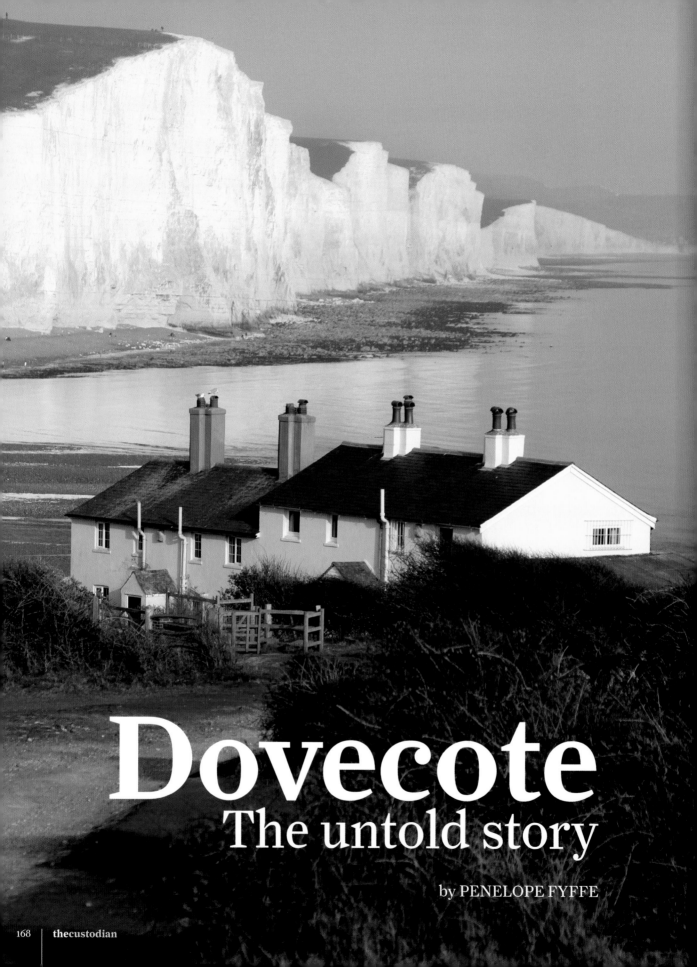

Dovecote
The untold story

by PENELOPE FYFFE

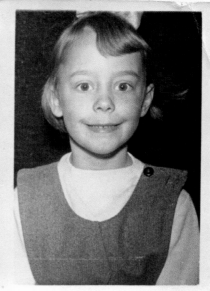

I can vividly remember the time when I first realised that my father was leading a double life. We were living in Pimlico, at 67 St George's Square, in a very grand Georgian white stucco wedding-cake that was way beyond our means.

Shortly after my eighth birthday, sister Marjorie and I were playing in the gardens with our nanny Emily, when a blond-haired cockney boy of about six or seven joined our little group. On realising who I was, he proclaimed:

''Eavens! So you're the Fyffe gel. Me dad lets me listen to 'is songs on the wireless. That *Bondage* one's a cracker!'

Over the coming months, as my father's reputation – and indeed, pocket book – grew, I was to learn that the man I called simply 'Daddy' was part of another family; the enormous, affectionate brotherhood of British music fans who, it seemed, had taken the simple songs of Brabbins and Fyffe straight to their hearts.

I remember vividly an enthusiastic taxi driver regaling my father and me with an industrious chorus of *I Wouldn't Touch Her With Yours*, or even more impressively, an entire tube carriage joyfully serenading us with the descant rejoinder from *More Than A Handful Is Wasted*.

Yet it was during the fateful hot summer of 1958 that my innocent bemusement at my father's wider sphere of influence gave way to a growing horror at the way he and his circle were choosing to live their lives. For this was the year in which they wrote the songs for which they were to become most famous, immortalised by their performance at the Fortune Theatre that October and captured forever in aspic as the world-famous long-player *Ship Shape and Bristol Fashion*. My father was at the peak of his creative powers; little was I to know his procreative powers weren't that far behind.

It was my father's partner in crime, the effusive Donald Brabbins, who suggested that their purpose in writing a new revue of songs might best be served in splendid isolation, the temptations of London living proving unconducive to the duo's efforts. Agents were dispatched and almanacs consulted, and Cuckmere Haven, just south of Eastbourne, was settled on as the perfect retreat.

As our brave little soot-grey Hillman Hunter mounted the bluff, and the whitewashed hunchback outline of Dovecote Cottage muscled its way into view, little were we to imagine the yawning chasm of chaos and existential oblivion that stretched Hades-like before us.

The first day passed solemnly enough. My father had shipped his infamous baby grand piano down from London and insisted on installing it in the kitchen, claiming it had by far the superior acoustic. My mother gave up all hope of being able to cook with the oven, and our meals instead became a rolling, mad hatter's tea party of barbecues and hastily convened salads. Meanwhile Donald Brabbins and my father would barricade the kitchen door and caterwaul and thump away, more as if they were working pig iron than fashioning popular songs.

But any such industry was short-lived. In the hustle and bustle of London life, the seedy underworld into which my father had been dragged was conveniently concealed; but here in plain view, it became horribly apparent to what depths the temptations of his inner darkness had led him.

On what was only the second morning of our residence, I woke early to a silent house, and tiptoed downstairs in my nightdress for a glass of milk. As I passed the sitting room, something stirred, and – my curiosity piqued – I decided to investigate. The long, thick floral-patterned curtains were closed, and the only source of light was from the dying embers of the grate.

Nevertheless I could make out what must have been a dozen or so female forms, draped upon one another in various states of *deshabillée*.

Their breathing was soft, but penetrated by a low creaking sound. Search as I might in the half-darkness, I failed entirely to discern where the sound was coming from, until by chance I happened to look up. The ceiling was inordinately high – one of the features of the house which I remembered had so impressed my father – and hanging from two sturdy bolts was the most enormous ~~contraption, the purpose~~ of ~~which~~ my ~~...~~ ~~...~~ ~~...~~ and my eyes widened in horror, for attached to the other end of it, comatose and with his voluminous beard matted with what can only have been his own emesis was the unmistakeable comatose form of Donald Brabbins, his eyes rolled back into the very ~~recesses~~ of ~~his~~ skull, and in his limp ~~...~~ grasp a ~~...~~ rending ~~...~~ all I could ~~...~~ bleach and oven glo~~ves~~.

With the last chord of that day's compostion still ringing in the air, my father would reach for what he called his 'medical kit'; a rough leather trunk that had been his constant companion since his ~~ev~~acuation during the second world ~~war~~. In it were closely packed all ~~man~~er of torniquets, rubber tubes, ~~...~~ glass phials, and powders, ~~...~~ for as my mother was later ~~...~~ ~~especi~~ally excited her to ~~...~~ ~~adm~~inistration ~~...~~

"Princess Margaret opened up the door to discover my father stark naked and holding a conductor's baton."

trick where Bertrand Russell made a tower of champagne glasses then created a fountain of flaming sambucca, setting fire to the footplate of Brabbins' wheelchair.

Indeed were it not for some deft work with a chemical fire extinguisher it is not impossible to conceive that fatalities ~~...~~ ~~...~~ ~~...~~ ~~...boggies.~~

Another frequent visitor was the delightful Diana Dors, fresh from her cinema hit *I Married A Woman*. As a young girl, the sight of this glamorous starlet with her chauffeur, her cut-glass vowels and her impossibly exotic hats and dresses was a vision to behold, and I quickly became her favourite, running and fetching for her, and endlessly pestering the cook for the tall glasses of lemonade she so liked to drink.

Imagine my horror and surprise, therefore, when on waking from one ~~of my~~ all-too-frequent night terrors ~~in~~ the dead of night, I padded down the back stairs to the kitchen with the intention of pouring myself a cool glass of water, only ~~to find the~~ young Miss Dors splay~~ed~~ ~~...~~ spatchcock on the ~~...~~ ~~...~~ kimbo, sm~~...~~ ~~...~~ Larry Adler, Lew Grade, and ~~...~~ Sellers looked on.

The Lord of Misrule, as ever, was Donald Brabbins, who at that moment appeared at the communicating doors carrying ~~a~~ ~~b~~ottle of castor oil whic~~h~~ ~~...~~ to smear all ov~~er~~ ~~...~~ ~~Miss~~ Dors' s~~...~~

Finally, impatient to say her goodbyes, Princess Margaret opened up the door to discover my father stark naked and holding a conductor's baton.

Before him were several of the young ladies she reco~~gnised from~~ ~~the Ch...~~ ~~...~~ different form of home-made animal mask and very little else.

As the young Princess murmured her startled apologies and backed out of the room, my father calmly took a deep draw on the hubble-bubble pipe before him and, on the exhale, explained that he had been teaching them the opening bars of Benjamin Britten's *Hymn To St. Cecilia*. Need~~les~~s to say a ~~...~~ ~~...~~ t sho~~...~~ a ~~...~~ ~~...~~ at which poi~~nt~~ ~~...~~ from the bac~~k~~ ~~...~~ ~~bu~~rst forth the quave~~ring~~ ~~...~~ ~~Pr~~incess Margaret striking ~~...~~ ~~...~~ ~~more~~ than a perfect top C, whic~~h she~~ ~~su~~stained seemingly effortlessly for a full eight bars.

An awed hush fell over us all. My father slowly lowered his baton, an expression of extreme surprise on his face. Princess Margaret paused for effect, and causally took a sip of Donald Brabbins' brandy, before handing it back to him with a cheeky wink.

'Right,' she pronounced, 'where are the marigolds? Someone's going to have to clean this mess up.'

And not for the last time in my life, I felt a huge burst of filial pride.

©Penelope Fyffe 2009

The Piano Man's Daughter by Penelope Fyffe is published by Armstrong, Miller on July 12th.

50 years on
What Brabbins & Fyffe meant to a generation

Professor Brian Cox

It's weird because they were like dead fuckin' posh, but I fuckin' love 'em, they had balls, at least Fyffe did. Not so sure about the other one, it's a bit of a fuckin' grey area in't it? What's the story there morning glory? Probably had a dodgy E, I know I fuckin' have, there's some right shite goin' round some of the lads at CERN, not sure what they fuckin' cut it with but it brought my stainless steel sink up a treat.

Anyway they made some great sounds and stuck it to the Man so all power to 'em. Did I mention I've started me own fuckin' clothing line? Buy sommat, don't buy sommat, it's all the same to me, so fuck ya. Right, I'm off to search through the debris of high-energy proton collisions for the signature of the Higgs Particle. Sound.

Robert de Niro

My father spent some time in England just after the war, and came into contact with their music through the owner of one of the galleries he exhibited in. When I was growing up in Little Italy, Manhattan, I would stay with him sometimes at his apartment. I would often lie awake while he worked, listening to these strange foreign voices drifting down the hallway and I guess it really stuck with me.

Years later, when I was playing the character of Michael in *The Deer Hunter*, before key scenes I would access some of that real close emotion by listening to a couple of minutes of *While You're Down There*. The audience, of course, should never be directly aware of an actor's preparation, though one sharp-eyed film fan did write me a nice letter saying she could see my foot tapping just before Nicky blows his brains out.

Stuart Maconie

So British in't it? I mean, one of them was in a wheelchair! I mean what's all that about? Can you imagine a singer being in a wheelchair these days!? Morrissey in a wheelchair next to Johnny Marr?! I don't think so! Dave Stewart in a wheelchair next to Annie Lennox?! I don't think so! Black Francis in a wheelchair next to Kim Deal? I don't think so! Bono in a wheelchair next to The Edge! I don't think so! In fact take any contemporary music act fronted by a notable duo, and imagine one of them in a wheelchair?! I don't think so!

Ross Kemp

It's a little known fact that I got my break in a Brabbins and Fyffe tribute act back in 1985 when I was fresh out of Mountview drama school. There had been at that time a revival of interest in their work thanks to a BBC documentary, presented, if I remember correctly, by Wayne Sleep.

Being something of a piano player I took the Teddy Fyffe role and a young Jimmy Nail assumed the mantle of the great Donald Brabbins. Six weeks later we had clocked up enough performances to get full Equity membership, and we both gained an enormous amount of respect for their achievements.

Years later, when I was filming *Ross Kemp In Afghanistan* in Helmand Province, the lads and I had a little bit of a drink one night and I came to in the officers' mess wearing nothing but a grass skirt and an L86A2 light support weapon, playing *Felching For Beginners* on an upright piano. Happy days.

Reader Offer

Here is your chance to be among the first to own a copy of the new digitally repolished Golden Jubilee Audiophile Edition of Brabbins & Fyffe's iconic 1959 album *Ship Shape and Bristol Fashion*. For the first time access has been granted to the original master tapes, and all twelve tracks, written during the notorious Dovecote sessions and still as relevant as ever, have been given extra sparkle and dynamic range by the latest digital technology.

As a special bonus, exclusive to **Custodian** readers, every copy will be accompanied by a highly detailed limited edition facsimile of the banned single *Seven Inches Suffice*, copies of which were the subject of a special Act of Parliament when subversive exhortations, apparently in the voice of Bertrand Russell, were claimed to have been hidden in the recording using so-called 'back-masking' techniques.

Produced on heavy-gauge archival vinyl, the record is fully playable, but also makes a striking piece of framable art.

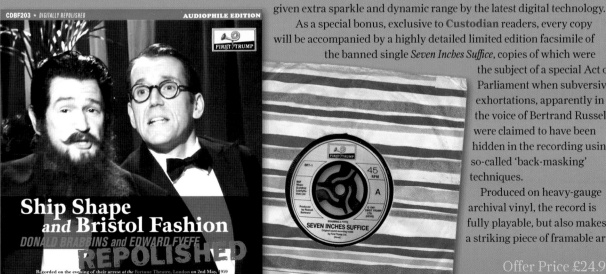

Offer Price £24.99

www.thecustodian.com/dovecote

Lonely? Depressed?

Be a teacher.

www.theyhavetolisten-itsthelaw.com

"Take a Break"

with some light-hearted drawings

You with your hand up. You need to keep rowing too.
You're risking our becalm-ment.

I'm afraid that ticket's expired, sir.
You'll have to apply for a new one.

They're a new form of slow release fish food. You drop
them in and they last for up to 18 hours.

I'm confused. I thought that meant I wouldn't be
able to see your repairs. I didn't realise it actually
meant that you yourself were invisible.

That'll teach you for suggesting I'm a fraud,
you fucking disrespectful bastard.

THE CRITICAL FACTOR
Television's Toughest Quiz

Gordon Brandt started his career in Belfast as a newspaper journalist and former UDF commander. After foreswearing paramilitary violence he joined local news programme *Ulster Reports* and also produced the popular comedy series *Titty Titty Bum Bum*. He came to Granada in 1974 and within a year he was fronting *The Critical Factor* – a new kind of quiz show. Gordon takes up the story ...

'Unlike other shows *The Critical Factor* tests many aspects of a contestant's abilities – mental agility, observation, general knowledge and physical aptitude. The stakes are higher too – in that those contestants failing to meet the challenges set out before them are expected to pay the ultimate price.'

'Some of the rounds have developed over

Since 1975, Monday nights at 7.00 have echoed with the popular catchphrase "Right, contestants – if you could turn to face the screens in front of you now and we'll commence the next round in a few moments' time."

That snappy sentence has been made famous by none other than Gordon Brandt – the stern yet moderately pleasant presenter of ITV's hit game show. And who better to show us around The Critical Factor studios and give us the inside track on TV's most unforgiving quiz!

the years and the physical endurance test has softened slightly. Contestants are no longer expected to hang by their thumbs for 40 seconds at the end of the assault course – but the basic format remains as it was at the start.'

'We're very proud of how efficient we are,' explains Gordon as he cleans the barrel of a Beretta 1201FP shotgun. 'Our kill rate is 100% with none of the unfortunate and messy accidents you see on other shows,' he says with a twinkle – a reference perhaps to the partial suffocation in the isolation booth that occurred in 1981 on the HTV husband and wife quiz show *Mr & Mrs*, which led to a thirty-eight-year-old woman entering a persistent vegetative state, where she resides to this day.

What does Gordon put this success down to? 'Our operatives are trained professionals with plenty of field experience – and over the years we've refined our methods. For example,

Left: Gordon with consultant civil engineer Christopher Oust, elated after victory in the endurance challenge, but soon to pay the ultimate price

Right: this year's popular winner, housewife Susan Small, still in robust health

contestants who go out on the general knowledge round are likely to find themselves on a conveyer line with their legs shackled and are then stunned with a captive bolt before final termination. It's clean, it's quick and it's humane.'

Given the popularity and longevity of the show, I wondered what changes Gordon had seen in his time as host. 'Well, we used to stun with the application of a low-voltage

Gordon's 'old faithful' Beretta, veteran of many elimination rounds

alternating current applied on either side of the cranium using tongs. But it sometimes took too long and could distract the contestants who hadn't been knocked out. Then we tried the Ranguiru system for a while, which is basically a modified electroplectic shock, but more recently we've switched to a less invasive method which involves the use of different concentrations of CO_2 gas. It only takes fifteen seconds,' says Gordon proudly.

CRITICAL FACTS

CRITICAL FACTOR

Five things you never knew about Gordon Brandt and the quiz he rules with an iron fist (and his team of enforcers)

As well as his TV career, Gordon Brandt owns a successful broccoli farm.

The Japanese have their own version of *The Critical Factor* – it's called *Anata no kenkou ni kanpai!* – which roughly translated means 'please take that cherry tree branch from my backside'.

The Royal Family are big fans of *The Critical Factor* and the Queen expects guests at Balmoral to watch it with her if they are staying on a Monday night.

Richard Drummie, the guitarist and singer with pop duo Go West – whose hits include 'We Close Our Eyes' and 'King of Wishful Thinking' – won the competition in 1982.

Gordon Brandt is related by marriage to George de Mestral, the inventor of Velcro.

BUILD & OPERATE YOUR OWN

You're sitting in the control room above the *Critical Factor* studio. Before you are banks of monitor screens and a large console by which you can keep in constant touch with the studio floor. Under your control are four cameras, coupled to monitors, a sound boom with microphone, a gallows, an electric chair, a fully operative guillotine, a sophisticated restraint couch and a Texas-style gas chamber. And, of course, you have a direct line to chairman Gordon Brandt himself, armed with a choice of police-issue tazer or Glock sub machine-gun.

You'll have hours of interest and fun cutting out the models below, glueing them together, lining up the cameras and cleanly and quickly planning how to end the lives of those that fail to meet the challenges set before them.

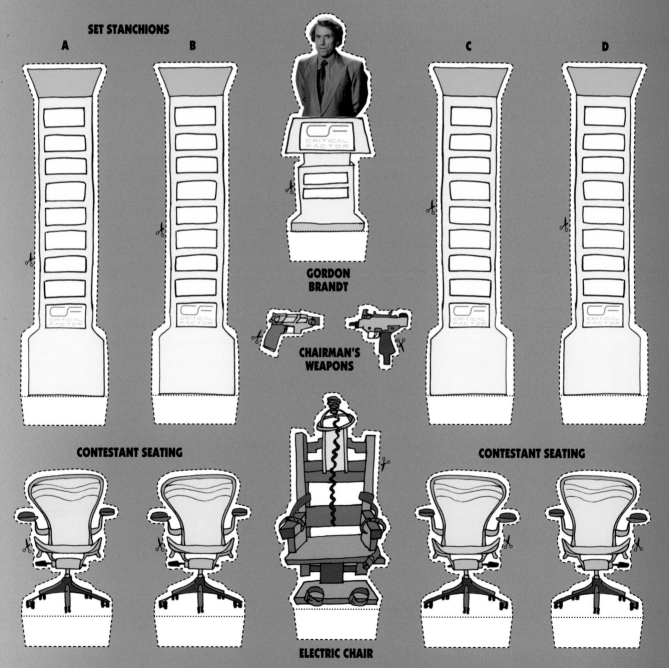

SET STANCHIONS

A B C D

GORDON BRANDT

CHAIRMAN'S WEAPONS

CONTESTANT SEATING

CONTESTANT SEATING

ELECTRIC CHAIR

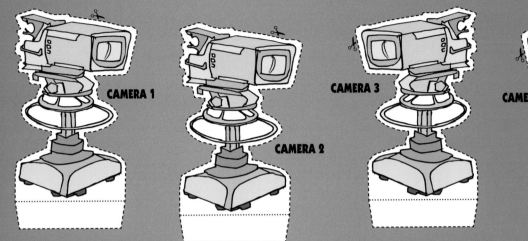

CAMERA 1

CAMERA 2

CAMERA 3

CAMERA 4

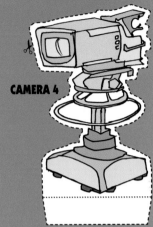

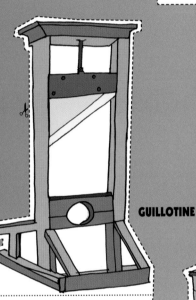

GUILLOTINE

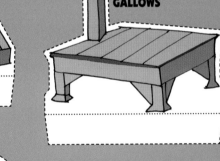

GALLOWS

Instructions for assembly

Paste each page on to stout cardboard, then, when completely dry, carefully cut out each component along the dashed lines. Fold back along the dotted lines to make a base to allow them to stand up freely. You will find that affixing one or two small copper coins to the base with sticky tape will improve stability.

RESTRAINT COUCH

GAS CHAMBER

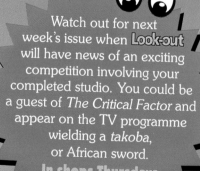

Watch out for next week's issue when **Look-out** will have news of an exciting competition involving your completed studio. You could be a guest of *The Critical Factor* and appear on the TV programme wielding a *takoba*, or African sword.

In shops Thursdays
ONLY 80p

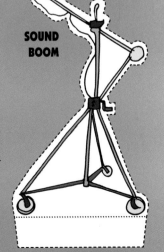

SOUND BOOM

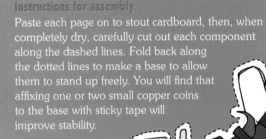

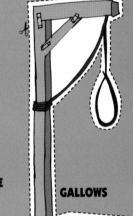

SHHHH!!!
I DO IT OLD SCHOOL

Classic Service.
Dewey Decimal system.
INDEX CARDS
DRAWER FILES

SILENCE
DEMANDED.

TRAMP IN CORNER
BY RADIATOR

DOWNSTAIRS

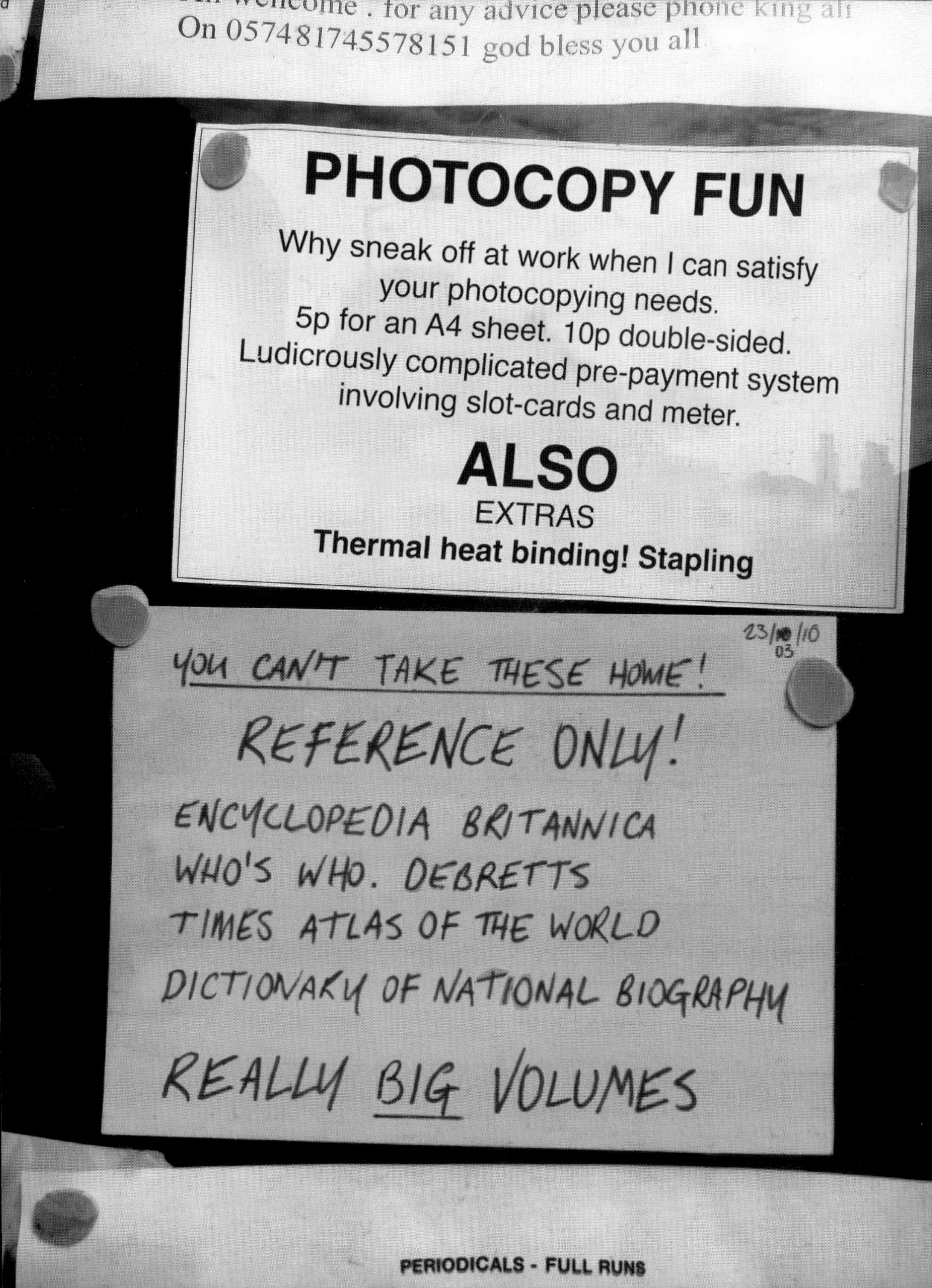

PHOTOCOPY FUN

Why sneak off at work when I can satisfy
your photocopying needs.
5p for an A4 sheet. 10p double-sided.
Ludicrously complicated pre-payment system
involving slot-cards and meter.

ALSO
EXTRAS
Thermal heat binding! Stapling

23/10/03

YOU CAN'T TAKE THESE HOME!

REFERENCE ONLY!
ENCYCLOPEDIA BRITANNICA
WHO'S WHO. DEBRETTS
TIMES ATLAS OF THE WORLD
DICTIONARY OF NATIONAL BIOGRAPHY

REALLY BIG VOLUMES

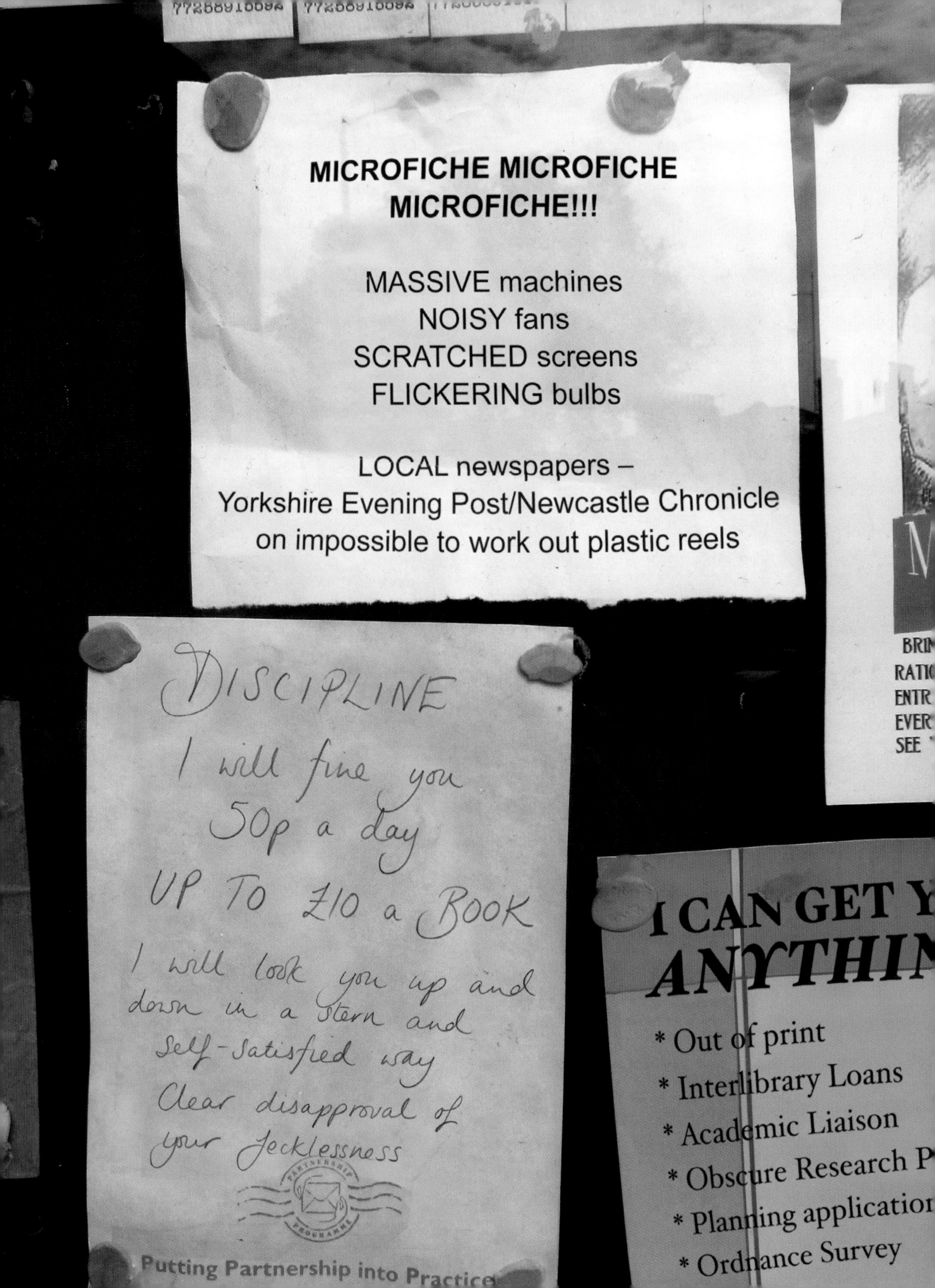

MICROFICHE MICROFICHE MICROFICHE!!!

MASSIVE machines
NOISY fans
SCRATCHED screens
FLICKERING bulbs

LOCAL newspapers –
Yorkshire Evening Post/Newcastle Chronicle
on impossible to work out plastic reels

DISCIPLINE

I will fine you
50p a day
UP TO £10 a BOOK

I will look you up and
down in a stern and
self-satisfied way
Clear disapproval of
your fecklessness

I CAN GET Y
ANYTHIN

* Out of print
* Interlibrary Loans
* Academic Liaison
* Obscure Research P
* Planning application
* Ordnance Survey

BRIM
RATIO
ENTR
EVER
SEE

http://www.biddencroft-pye.ltd.uk

nice hole puncher

Biddencroft & Pye

EST. 2008

FINEST ●RGANIC IR●N H●LE-PUNCHES

Each Biddencroft & Pye organic hole-punch is hand assembled and spot welded at Cherry Weather Farm in the middle of Dorset's most attractive trading estate.

Only once our team of craftsmen and skilled workers is satisfied that each one passes a range of stringent and exacting checks will the hole-punches be sent through to our organic hand-painting workshop. Here our paint captains (all of them members of the Worshipful Guild of Master Metal-painters) lavish every care and effort to apply our patented low-carbon-footprint hammered enamel finish.

The result – we feel sure you'll agree – is worth all the care, attention, effort and pride we put into our hole-punches.

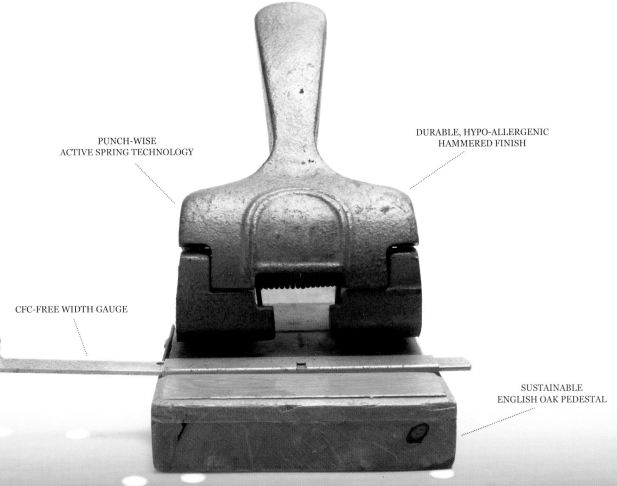

PUNCH-WISE
ACTIVE SPRING TECHNOLOGY

DURABLE, HYPO-ALLERGENIC
HAMMERED FINISH

CFC-FREE WIDTH GAUGE

SUSTAINABLE
ENGLISH OAK PEDESTAL

Biddencroft & Pye Organic Hole-Punches.
There's n●thing m●re t● say.

L●●K ●UT *for our stand at ShitFest 2011*

Baron Anton Von Schleisinger
van Hoeken-Hoek von Horschstadt
Undead, 872

"You need one high-impact piece
and then your look is solid."

Cloak, dyed with the blood of
virgins, vintage; wool suit,
Turnbull & Asser S/S 1926,
approx 200 guineas; cilice
(not visible), silver-gilt
and enamel, gift from Pope
Gregory IX; neck piece, one-off
by "a St. Martin's student,
I forget her name"; white
shirt, George at Asda, £8.

PHOTOGRAPHY » Waller
STYLING » Timmy B
MAKEUP » models' own

**High Prince
Alto Pharius The Dread**
Undead, 2,475

"I like classics with a twist;
I'll accessorise something
Coptic or Etruscan with a
bang-up-to-date cummerbund from
the Weimar Republic, whatever
works."

Embroidered overmantle from
a selection at the court of
King Ludwig II, £POA; buttoned
tunic, pillaged; blouse (worn
as skirt), "ripped from prey";
white shirt, Uniqlo, £16;
chrysoprase ring, Bohemian,
made to order.

INSTRUCTIONS
FOR
ITISH SERVICEMEN
IN
GERMANY

Prepared by
e Political Warfare Executive

Issued by
The Foreign Office,
London

AND PHRASES—

Hey, blud. Who am dat?	Halt! Wer da? *halhlt vair dah*
Reach for it, remtard!	Hände hoch! **henda** *hohk*
Is it that you has any papers and this? (NB *in this case papers isn't like them papers what you use for rolling jazzy fags and that*)	Geben Sie mir Ihre Papiere **gay**ben *zee meer eera* **papeer**a
Out the way	Entschuldigen Sie ent**shool**diggen *zee*
What?	Verzeihung *fair***tsyoong**
Any of you massive gaylords know how to talk?	Spricht jemand english? *shprisht* **yay**mant **eng**lish
Soz, gotta go	Ich habe es eiligwich **hah**ba *es* **eye**lish
Watch out, rasclart!	Achtung! or Vorsicht! **ahk**toong! **fore**zisht!
Stay here	Warten Sie hier, bitte **vahr**ten *zee here* **bitta**
Don't lose your shit, man. Is you some kind of girl or something? Isn't it?	Keine Angst **kyna** angst
What?	Wiederholen Sie es *veeder***hoh**len *zee ess*
What?	Ich verstehe nicht *ish fair***shtaya** *nisht*
What?	Was wollen Sie? *vahss* **voll**en *zee?*
What?	Was ist los? *vahss ist lohs?*
Hear me now military bredren, I is saying nothing	Ich weiss nichts davon *ish vice nishts da***fon**
Where's you shootin' me fam?	Wo gehen Sie hin? *vo* **gay**en *zee hin*
I hasn't a clue where I is going and shit	Ich habe den Weg verloren *ich* **hah**ba *dain vaik fair***loh**ren
Soz, blud, got another call coming through, isn't it?	Ich kann hetzt nicht mit Ihnen sprechen *ich khan yetst nisht* *mit* **een**en **shpres**hen
You know staying here? Yeah? You know staying? Yeah? Staying? That? That Thing? Staying, yeah? You know that? Well, can you not?	Bitte gehen Sie weg *bitta* **gay**en *zee veck*
I'm gonna like shoot, yeah? And then I'm gonna all like come back? Isn't it?	Ich komme später zurück *ish* **komm**a **shpat**er *tsoo***rick**

WARMONGER ... continued from page 40

PLUCKY 'B' SQUADRON TAKE TO THE SKIES OVER DOVER AND PREPARE TO MEET THE MIGHTY LUFTWAFFE ...

Sunray to Base ... Altitude 9,000 ft heading due east. When can we expect contact ... over?

You should see them any second ... over!

UP AHEAD ...

Sunray to Base. No sign of them ... over!

TO BE CONTINUED ON PAGE 323 ...

CARELESS TALK COSTS NOTHING

IF YOU IS ON THE RIGHT TARIFF

Dvobe Chair
Rosenblatt's celebrated pastiche of office comfort stock. Complete with castors, full swivel and lumbar support. Hilarious.
Theo Rosenblatt
www.truk.sw
£ Fuck Off

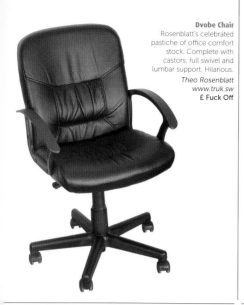

The Pharaoh
This armchair with giltwood bingo wings and exquisite armscroll tassels looks almost too good to be true. Has a human *really* made something this beautiful? Or a God? You decide.
Marcus Thackeray, 52 Sloane Avenue, SW3
www.marthack.co.uk
£ Fuck Off

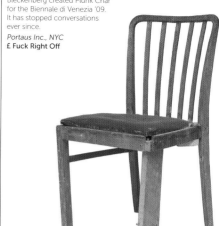

Plunk Char
Bleckenberg created Plunk Char for the Biennale di Venezia '09. It has stopped conversations ever since.
Portaus Inc., NYC
£ Fuck Right Off

Nayassi Okogommi/ Shut Up And Sit Down
The marmite of Okogommi's oeuvre, you either love it or would rip out and eat your own heart to own it.
U B Inkermann & Sons, Rennes
£ I Can't Believe You're Still Looking At This – Fuck Off

Alfresco
Commissioned by Alessandro Beshcato for the Palazzo San Paulini. Only twelve of these were made.
Portaus Inc., NYC
£ How Did You Even Get Hold Of This Magazine? Fuck Off

Tallulah
Kosmo Stephini takes the bar-fly theme and sends it to college. And back it comes *magna cum laude*. Sit on this and weep.
Benkhaus, Gstaad
£ This Is Now Virtual Trespass. Fuck Off Or I'll Turn Nasty

Quadruped
The winner of the Prix Gourgette at Milan. Gryphon hide and white gold.
Glock, Madrid
£ Far Cough

Bale by Alastair Geffen
The straw that broke the camel's back in Dubai last year when Geffen took diamond in the *Fête Furn-être*.
Geffen Studios, London
£ It's Made Of Straw, Maybe We Could Afford That. No, The Twine's Made of Gold, So Fuck Off

Dog Chair
In Azure. Sebastian Farnborough's *Picnic With Dangerous Breeds* series. A modern classic.
sit, Pimlico, London
£ How Can I Put This In A Way You'll Understand? If The Value Of Your House Is A Pinhead, This Is The O₂. You Know, What Used To Be The Dome. Is That Any Clearer?

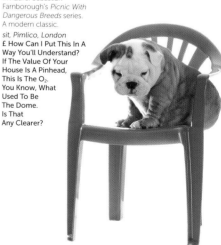

Kyoto N+2
Sesshu Motonobu has caught the chair world's eye with this stripped-down lacquered pine sit-piece. Heaven.
Ponuta Shop, Ginza, Tokyo
£ Come On Off You Fuck

iMac Chair
Exceptional calf-leather comfort in puce. This Steve Jobs-commissioned rarity still dazzles one decade on.
Sit Up And Beg, Firenze, Italia
£ Turn The Page Povvo You Can't Afford This

Mache Dich
Pendenny's scathing attack on the sedentary axis. Only now available after a seventeen-year blackout.
Christie's New York Contemporary Chair Sale, 17 April
£ Get The Fuck Outta Here

The Fauntleroy
Another Marcus Thackeray design classic – ambrosia rendered as soft furnishing.
Marcus Thackeray, 52 Sloane Avenue, SW3
£ Imagine How Much Money Your Family And Friends Could Raise If They Had To, You Know, Like When Someone Has To Have An Operation – Well, Imagine If You Put All That Money On A Horse That Came From Nowhere To Win The Grand National And You Go To Pick Up The Winnings All Happy And Everything Cos Everything's Going To Be Alright ... Well It's Not Enough, So Fuck Off

The Lynda
Riesenschfal's wry take on 50s pod furniture. Absolutely not for sitting on.
sit, Pimlico, London
£ Go A-Fucking Way

The Big Bold Print Fly-Trap Chair
This deceptively inexpensive-looking chair draws you in by looking like it's from DFS. Like fuck it is.
Davide LaPrince, Los Angeles
$ Fuck Off (And That's In Fucking Dollars, Lazarus, Even Before You've Shipped The Motherfucker Over From LA [That's In America]. Do You Know Any Shippers? Do You? Thought Not.) Fuck Off

Troll Chair
When Cooper Seaberg and Michel Sandbach collaborated in the 1980s, no one could have known that this acme of design, mathematics, and sheer physical beauty would be the result.
Spelmous Inc., Chicago
£ Alright How Much Do You Want? How Much For You To Fuck Off?

A standout selection of seatware is available at the Pimlico showrooms of **sit**. It's hard to believe that these beautiful pieces also fulfil a function as furniture, but as **sit**'s proprietor **Matthew Boude** tells me, it's all a matter of where you sit on the form-versus-function *fauteuil* ...

sit!
Fuck Off Chairs

It means so much to the two of us that all of you are here to share in our special day.

Please use this book to leave us a personal record of any well-wishes, inner wisdom, or personal feelings that you would like to share with us.

Jim & Dee

PLEASE RETURN to BEST MAN !!!

THANK GROOM FOR HIS TOAST

THANK THE PARENTS

TOAST THE PARENTS

Ben	Dear Tim an... We've b... both of y... Can't w...
Steve & Mona	What a lovely occasion! Thank you for letting us share in your celebrations, and best of luck to you both in the future. Love × × × ×
Adam & Tamara	Jim & Jen – Welcome to the club! Thanks for a great day! ××
Fabia	Congratulations! Thanks for inviting us to share this special day with you. All our best wishes for a long & happy marriage! Love, Fabia + Martin ×

Dear Jim and Jen —
MAZELTOV on such a fantastic day.
The bride never looked more lovely.
And so good that the weather held up.
x Nick and Teresa.

Nick.

To Jim + Jen,
Congratulations to you both — and may the
sun shine on your marriage!
Love & best wishes to you both. x

Diane
+ Steve

To the happy couple!
Congratulations on your special day
I know you'll have a wonderful
life together! With all my love

My.

FUNNY STORIES ABOUT EX - GIRLFRIENDS

1. Julie - he drank bleach after

2. Kerry - restraining order

3. Jackie - self-harm with tenon saw

Jim,
to you both and thank
iting me to share this

NICE THINGS ABOUT JEN:
- loves her, meant to be together
PROPOSE TOAST TO JEN
TELEGRAMS / EMAILS
CHECK JIM HAS TAKEN MEDICATION

From: JimTallon@solihull.gov.uk
Subject: Suggested song list
Date: 21 June 2010 16:17:09 GMT+01:00
To: matt.d@souldiscoinferno.biz
Cc: <Jen>JennyParfitt@solihull.gov.uk

hey matt,

dont want to tread on your blue suede wheels of steel but here are some jen-n-jim rock solid classics which I know will go down a storm.
but up to you, mate - youre the dj wid da mad skillz so anything you can throw down to make it a day to remember will be just what the doctor ordered. except the first dance - thats non-negotiable!

every breath you take ill be watching you-sting
(first dance)
too shy-kajagoogoo
the best is yet to come-old blue eyes
ive had the time of my life-bill medley & jennifer warnes
unbreakable-westlife
we've only just begun-carpenters
nothings going to stop us now-starship

its gonna be a roadblock!!!! see you saturday. no disco biscuits friday night if you don't mind!
just kidding.

Jim Tallon

Sarah

Dear Jim and Jen

Many congratulations - Jen, your dress was beautiful and you looked a picture! Here's to a long and happy life together. All my love, Sarah xx

Mel.

Dear Jen & Jim - all the very best on your special day - Enjoy!

Mel, David & the girls x

Dear Jen,

CONGRATULATIONS! Just wandered into the back of the dance tent and saw you DEEP THROATING the DJ. Took him really far back without bringing up any of that BEEF Wellington you were so keen on us having for the WEDDING supper.

Thank goodness we didn't go with the fish! HAPPY DAYS!

Your loving husband, Jim

P.S. I don't think we're going to get the deposit back on the marquee. Not now it's throwing up fifty foot flames and melting the rubber on the overHEAD power line!!!

We're in love ...   Tom & Inès Ligamamada-Teach

Inès: Shut up, Tom! You always talk too much! You like monkey –
chatter, chatter, chatter – you give me big headache. Why you not be
quiet so I can tell it to the lady? I so sorry, Tom is really bad manners,
he is like big hairy pig honk honk honk.

Inès: Tom! Tom! TOM! Fetch me white wine spritzer! Yes yes with ice! I only like with the ice. Honestly, he is so stupid!

Inès: So anyway, we meet long long time ago when I live in Spice Islands. I always say, I am one of SPICE GIRLS – ha ha ha ha ha! I was very beautiful, very beautiful, my hair so beautiful, all the men and the boys they want to marry me, but I say no because I want to – TOM! I want now! Spritzer! Honestly, he is so stupid, like tiny ant which forget all the time which way is it going?!

Inès: Anyway, I was very beautiful, like flower, and one day big ship come in to harbour, with black sails and my sister Carmenza she say, 'Look, Inès, look pirate' and I see Tom step ashore and I say to her, 'So what? No big deal!' Is true, first time I see him I think he look like little badger, like little badger with tiny eyes and little white hands. 'He not like man,' I say to her, 'he like a boy! Like a little tiny boy!!'

I did say that, didn't I, Tom?!!

Tom? Tom!!! TOM!!! TOOOOOMMM!!! Put it here!!! Mmmm – lovely spritzer I love so much! SO much!!! Wine so tasty!!

Inès: But Tom he crazy about me and he give me gold and jewels and he say: 'Come to England and we will be happy' and I not want to go but he beg me and I feel sorry for him, he look so sad like chicken with no beak because of disease hahahaha!!!! It true I see one like that one time!!! Look at Tom, he listen, haha – look his face hahahaha!!

Inès: So we travel on boat and we get married in equator and I so please because now I can eat what I want and I want A LOT!!!! Tom!! TOM!!! Wake up!! He stare out of the window all the time like that – it drive me crazy.

Inès: Anyway we come to Portsmouth and I choose nice house with nice carpet and nice utility room and nice garden and Tom he so happy!!! One day he say to me Inès I no want to be pirate no more, and I say good for you Tom Teach. He say: 'I much more happy stay home with you and watch TV or go to cinema and laugh at Jennifer Aniston movie.' He build new kitchen for me next week. He love so much the house we choose from IKEA and everything. I so proud of him!!! I think he happiest he ever be in whole life???!!!! Is not that right Tom Teach??!! Tom. Tom! Tom!! TOM!!! WHY YOU NEVER LISTEN YOU LIKE STUPID STUPID STUPID STUPID STUPID MAN!!!!

Tom: Arrr.

*Tom and Inès were talking to **Rosie Montague***

'He so happy.
I know is true
ahahahaha!'

Lateral urban living on a Titanic scale
Salcombe

Kingsbridge: 6 miles, A30 Dual Carriageway: 15 miles, London (Paddington): 2 hrs 50 mins

almost 3,000 sq ft with an additional 1,000 sq ft of decked balcony • 3 reception rooms • ooh, this sounds affordable, doesn't it? it's not even in London • yeah? try this for size • 6/7 bedrooms • boom • 300 sq ft staff flat • boom • double garage • do you have two cars? • thought not • boom • large private garden • private, yeah? like this house is meant to be • so fuck off

Guide: £ Just Fuck Off

Fuck Off
Urban

www.fuckoffurban.com

Backside Boys

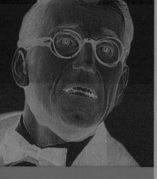

donnie **BRABBINS** & ed **FYFFE**

RED ROAR DAY

Sixties swingers Brabbins & Fyffe are back in the charts with a classic track re-issued for Red Roar Day, in aid of victims of corporal punishment. This week's #27.

THE CLOSER ONE GETS TO WIFEY
THE LESS HEAT ONE MAY FEEL
BUT THANKFULLY
    THERE ARE WAYS AND MEANS
    TO STIMULATE RELATIONS
ALL YOU NEED IS A BIT OF PLUCK
    AND A LEWD IMAGINATION ...

OH A LITTLE BIT OF BONDAGE
    GOES A LONG LONG WAY
SOME MILD HUMILIATION
    AND RESTRAINT WILL SAVE THE DAY

YES A LITTLE BIT OF BONDAGE
    GOES A LONG LONG WAY

TO KEEP THE MARRIAGE BED ON FIRE
    TRY SOME PLAYFUL DEPILATION
I'VE HAD HOURS OF FUN FOR FREE
    WITH A BOWL OF SOAPY WATER
    AND A FRESH GILLETTE MACH3

OR EXPERIMENT WITH HANDCUFFS
AND A BUZZING TOY OR TWO ...
THOUGH BE CAREFUL NOT TO
    WAKE
        THE
            KIDS

YES A LITTLE BIT OF BONDAGE
    GOES A LONG LONG WAY

a little bit of BONDAGE

OH A LITTLE BIT OF BONDAGE
    GOES A LONG LONG WAY
SOME MILD HUMILIATION
    AND RESTRAINT WILL SAVE THE DAY

YOU COULD TRY A TOUCH OF SPANKING
CORPORAL PUNISHMENT ROLE PLAY
I LIKE TO BE THE SQUIRE
    (AND I LIKE TO BE THE MAID)
MIX IT UP TO
    KEEP
        THINGS
           HOT

ONE CAN GO A LITTLE FURTHER
IF ONE'S TASTE IS SO INCLINED
SCRAPE YOUR KNOB ACROSS A GRATER
NORMALLY USED FOR LEMON RIND

OH THERE REALLY ARE NO LIMITS
TO MAN'S EROTIC MIND ...
APART FROM THOSE
    PROSCRIBED
        IN
           LAW

YES A LITTLE BIT OF BONDAGE
    GOES A LONG LONG WAY
THOUGH WE HAVE A WORD OF CAUTION
THAT WE'LL PASS ON IF WE MAY ...

YOU CAN FEEL QUITE SOILED AND DIRTY IN
THE MORNING COME THE LIGHT ...
BUT THAT'S HOW YOU KNOW YOU'VE
    GOT
        IT
           RIGHT

REPEAT REFRAIN TO FADE

WORDS AND MUSIC BY BRABBINS/FYFFE
REPRODUCED BY PERMISSION
(C) TRUMP RECORDINGS 1961
(P) TEDDY TUNES

Backside Boys say:
'Don't forget
Red Roar Day this Thursday.'
A whopping 13½p goes to charity
for every 'Bondage' 7" sold.

THE ADVENTURE
OF THE UNEASY ENCOUNTER[1]

I HAD SEEN LITTLE of Holmes lately. My practice was busier than ever and its demands absorbed all my attention. Holmes—who loathed every form of society with his whole Bohemian soul—remained in our old lodgings in Baker Street, doubtless buried among his dusty books and alternating from week to week between cocaine and ambition.

From time to time I heard tell of some vague account of his doings—not that I had the slightest interest in any of them. There was the summons to St Petersburg in the case of the Ivory Elephant.[2] Or his clearing up of the singular tragedy of the Enniskillen Kipper.[3] Or even the mission which he had accomplished so delicately and successfully, hushing up for the Vatican.[4]

One night (it was the thirteenth of April to be precise[5]) I just happened to be passing—completely accidentally—221b Baker Street. I paused to untie my shoelace—spending an extra minute untying and retying my other shoe lace just to make sure it, too, wouldn't come undone—only to glance up and see Holmes' tall, spare figure pass twice, a dark silhouette against the blind. He was pacing the room swiftly, with his head sunk upon his chest and his hands clasped behind him. He looked like he was lonely, perhaps regretting the fact

1 "The Adventure of the Uneasy Encounter" was published in the *Strand Magazine* in February 1898 and in *Harper's Weekly* (New York) on 15 April, 1989.

2 A Russian Count—a distant relative of the Tzar—had been found impaled upon said item's tusks. They passed in through the sternum and out through the belly.

3 A country doctor had been slowly poisoned by mercury-laden herrings, provided by his mistress.

4 Unbelievably a whole raft of priests and cardinals had been falsely accused of mass pederasty.

5 Coincidentally this was the seventh anniversary of Holmes and Watson first taking up rooms together.

Dr. Watson & Mr. Torrance

6 Although Holmes *was* a keen practical joker—once arranging for a Georgian terraced house to be rebuilt around a hippopotamus he had hired from the Zoological Gardens in Regents Park.

7 The career of Emmett Torrance was marked out by a series of blunders, most notably when he mistook Princess Feodora—Queen Victoria's half-sister—for Sarah Mann, a notorious East End prostitute.

8 Watson now kept rooms with Emmett Torrance in Pimlico Road, above a Chapel of Rest (which Torrance had mistaken for a bed-shop when he took the lease).

that he now lived on his own, something he must have felt particularly keenly given that I had taken up rooms with another gifted detective—one Emmett Torrance.

Squatting there—behind a pillar box simply to keep out of the wind—I thought it would be amusing to play a trick on Holmes, given how notoriously lacking his sense of humour could so often be.[6] I reached for a handful of gravel and threw it at his study window. After a moment, the sash flew up.

"I know it's you, Watson."

I said nothing, pressing my back tight against the cast iron railing.

"You're such a predictable creature."

There was a pause in which I said nothing.

"What's the matter? Has Torrance been finally incarcerated for terminal stupidity?"[7]

"Now who's being predictable?" I couldn't help but reply. There was another testy pause.

"Well come in if you're coming. I've told Mrs Hudson to expect you, given the date," he added drily. "Life in Belgravia[8] clearly suits you. You've put on eight-and-a-half pounds."

"Eight," I retorted. For some reason I felt myself blush.

"I see I've touched a raw nerve," he said, as he stoked the dying fire, the slightest grin playing around his narrow lips. "Not getting the exercise you once did? Fieldwork not really Torrance's thing?"

"Don't start," I said, finding myself drawn to my old familiar chair to the right of the hearth.

⤙⬦⬦

WE ATE SUPPER in a desultory silence which—eventually—Holmes broke.

"Why are you here, Watson? Hmmm?"

"*You* asked me in. Why do you think I'm here?"

Holmes put down the salt cellar he had been shaking aimlessly over his game pie.

"Because it is in the nature of desire to want what you haven't got," he said coolly.

I flashed him a look.

"I'm sorry. I'm sorry," he apologised, before swiftly changing the subject. "I have a new case. A stolen racehorse. You always loved the races.[9] Why not come with me? Tomorrow."

"I must leave," I said, standing up. "Emmett is waiting. We have an investigation to review."

Surprising me, Holmes hand snaked out and grasped mine.

"So much pain. Scratch an inch—my dearest Watson—a fraction of an inch and you're in it. It's nothing to bring it to mind, is it? Nothing."

"Fuck off, Holmes," I ejaculated, "you pompous, self-regarding shit." And I left, making my way out into the cold spring night.

9 Watson was a keen racegoer—unusually, for a man of his background, enjoying dog racing as much as horse—but he gave the latter up after once attending with Torrance, who was overheard wondering how they would find "jockeys tiny enough to ride them".

TH
T

80/20 WOOL BLEND

MANUFACTURED IN THE UK

ARMSTRONG/MILLER
LAMINATES

Grandeur

25

12

EXTRA LONG &
WIDE PLANKS

v-groove

true to
nature
touch

chrome
zone

AC-4

CE

KEN'S CARPETS

Est. 1979
Prop. Kenneth D. Carpets FRSCF

E GOOD BOOK
E FLOORCOVERING BIBLE

The 2 Fold Way

The most important factor in carpet quality.

Each tuft of an Armstrong & Miller carpet has 2 ends of yarn. The doubling of the fine ends of yarn makes for a finer finish GIVING SUPERIOR QUALITY, RESILIENCE & DURABILITY AND PREVENTING PILE REVERSAL.

THE CARPET
FOUNDATION

"Carpet Diem"

FINE 2-FOLD YARNS PREVENT PILE REVERSAL, GIVING
ER APPEARANCE RETENTION, RECOVERY AND RESILIENCE

**clean
air**

**BREATH
EASIER**
with carpets by
Armstrong
& Miller

Scientific Research
shows that carpet
improves indoor

MINSTREL Colour: Tarbouka

This is a life saver. I've turned to the old Mins/Tarb many, many times. On the occasion that I visited the doc and he give it to me straight that I would never achieve erection I laid nearly fifteen hundred square of the beautiful stuff.

HANBURY CARE PLAIN Colour: Parish

This one's my little Paul Ince – that's what I call it! He runs in from nowhere, covers the whole field and makes sense out of whatever rubbish was there before. Dear oh dear, I'm tearing up now.

RECITAL Colour: Schubert

Phil was having a problem with his little girl. She'd been seeing someone who didn't cut the mustard powder. Must be quite annoying if you feel strongly about your condiments. Anyway, I sweep in like Sir Galahad with the Recital in her bedroom. Boy's gone next day.

INTUITION Colour: Oversley

After Executive Parlsey, the Oversley Intuition is my most dependable floor-covering. I know it will always be there for me: winter, spring, summer or fall as the song says. Doesn't need a pile neither cos it's so serenely knotted you feel like you're walking on sunshine. I'm doin' all the songs today!

VARSITY Colour: Raindrop Blue

I laid this in our bedroom the day after Shoneeza said, 'I will,' so that it would always feel like a starlit night in there. And do you know? It always does. Sometimes I take Shoneeza in my arms and then we leave it there cos I can't achieve erection.

DUET NOVA Colour: Sky Blue

Do you know what this unassuming little patch of wool-mix says to me? It says, 'Oy Ken, when you gonna get on the blower to Phil about that hall carpet of his? It'll not do another year, eighteen months tops.' Alright, I say, I'll call him tomorrow.

Specify with Confidence

PALLADIUM Colour: Dark Blue

When my old ma passed on – must've been fifteen year ago – I took the old book of magic out to the park and sat in quiet communion with my little samples for the best part of a day. They're like tiny glimpses of the different directions your life might take and ... oh, listen to me – sentimental old bugger!

PRECISION Colour: Regal

I was watching the old Trooping the Colour on the box the other day and I could've sworn the flag they was carrying around was made of this stuff. Bloody beautiful it was. Then I noticed it's called Regal Precision. How d'you like that?! I've called the Queen's secretary and offered to run up a couple for next year!

EVESHAM Colour: Avon

Avon Evesham seems to be saying 'Hello, how are ya?' but reading between the knots it's actually got a darker side. A carpeting of surprising depth and oh my goodness this one wears hard. Very hard. Your great grandkids'll still be loving this one.

ACROPOLIS Colour: Aristotle Blue

It's only right they name this stunning floor covering after a philosopher because it is to the Aristotle Blue Acropolis that I turn for the more profound answers. What do I want out of life? How can I be a better person? How do I change wholesaler without giving Shirty Ahmed the hump?

COMPILATION Colour: Bluebell

Look into this little patch and try to let your eyes relax focus so you're gazing into it and about a foot or two 'beyond'. Are you starting to see it? I see the shape of – hang on it's gone. Normally I get him off the X-Factor. Little Irish one.

CREATION Colour: Cosmos

I often wonder if you could make clothes out of carpet, cos if you could then I would have a car-coat of Cosmos Creation run up for me, and I don't think you'd ever get it off my back. See how the little ferrous flecks of orange play through the palette? I don't think I've seen a lovelier thing. Ever.

Specify with Confidence

InternationalCollection

Burnt Oak

I could always lay a bit of Burnt Oak for you if that's what you really wanted. Burnt Oak though? Are you sure? Feel it and think of the splinters. I'll do it – I'm just saying.

Rustic Oak

You know why they call it Rustic Oak? Cos it's reconditioned. Put this down and two years, three years down the line you'll have warping and rising next to the rads. Just saying.

English Hickory

I despair with some of this stuff because you'll notice they always call it a hard wood ('oak', 'hickory') when in fact it's just veneered pine. Pretty sure that's veneered pine. Listen, I'm very happy to fit it for you if that's what you want.

Japanese Cherry

Oh, very nice. Japanese Cherry. I should imagine the Japanese cherry is very delectable to eat. But *flooring*? You want to walk on a bit of fruit wood? Well, it's up to you of course.

Austrian Oak

Tell you what, you'd feel like you was living in one of them Austrian saunas if you had this underfoot. I'd keep expecting to see some naked man with a blonde moustache walk in ha ha ha ha! Your choice of course.

New Zealand Birch

I will grant you this is a beautiful colour for a flooring but it's not right. Just look at the Horseradish Launceston on the second to last page. The Launceston's never going to scuff. This one's gonna look like 101 Dalmations after a week. But I'll gladly put it in if that's what you want.

Specify with Confidence

STRATOSPHERE

This is a cloth of gold, a wheat field, a gilded skein of braided barley dazzling as it dances in the magic light at the end of a drowsy summer's day. It's on special too so it's a bargain.

MARRAKECH

I've never been to Morocco – never seen the point to be honest with you. If you know Tunis like I do it's just another stamp in the bleedin' passport. However, I go to Marrakech like a pilgrim every time I open this book. And what goes on tour, stays on tour.

INDIAN GOLD

This is the Brahmin of the Good Book – an historic weft of sub-continental culture and ancient wisdom. Like any gold it will hold its value and like any generous tuft it'll hold tight to its gripper rods. A magic carpet.

POPPYSEED

This one is the Get Out Of Jail card in my tarot deck. It means freedom. It's a picnic hamper full of night-time, it's a Shreddie after lights-out, it's Manhattan from the sky. Walk on it and become a citizen of the world. Sorry, just had a bit too much coffee.

NEW COLOURS

SEE HANGING SAMPLES

LATE FLOWERING LUST

This one is not for the kids – in fact I'm not laying this in sight of anyone under 21. I thought long and hard about stocking something as downright pornographic as this and I'll be honest I'm still uneasy about it. I am inured against it to some degree of course (because I can't achieve erection) but it still gets me.

Specify with Confidence

Scraped a maths GCSE?

Be a teacher.
www.nobastardwantstoteachmaths.com

Do you enjoy being a meter man?
Is it interesting work?

We need to search your property, madam. We've reason to
believe a serious crime is being planned from these premises.

Squawk squawk squawk.

Chuckle Corner

....

It's entertaining
because it's true

Watch yourself! That looks painful.

Neither myself or my wife are interested in
purchasing an encyclopedia, thank you.

Flint & Rory's

REALLY WILD

COOK OUT!

Out & About:
Hunting Down the Good Life

Dead Tasty

Have your wicked way with carrion and roadkill

As everyone knows, **the real art of cooking** lies in using all the ingredients you have available and making sure nothing **gets wasted**. And when you're cooking in the wild, half the trick is knowing what you can find! Well, there's a whole game-larder full of varied free-range, organic meats that you can raid as often as you like and guess what? It's all **ABSOLUTELY FREE**. That, dudes, is the joy of roadkill!

Quite often you'll find the meat has been gutted, filleted and **spatch-cocked** already so all you need to do is to pick out the gritty bits, lop off the chunks you don't fancy and whack it on to the old camping stove with a lug of olive oil and **VIOLA** (as my old music teacher used to play).

Rabbits, game birds, roe deer, muntjac – we all know how **DELICIOUS** these are sizzling in the pan, but the real roadside treats are the unexpected ones: **badger** (which tastes somewhere between wild boar and venison!), **squirrel** (chicken!), **stoat** (between chicken and wild boar!), **vole** (badger and wild boar!) and **otter** (stoat and vole!).

SORTED!

Now, quite how **adventurous** you want to be depends on various factors like a) how **hungry** are you? b) how **squeamish** are you? and c) is there a decent **Waitrose** on the ring-road of the nearest town? The first rule of wild cooking is try everything once but **never make yourself eat anything YOU DON'T LIKE THE LOOK OF**.

And the thing about roadkill is you have **no way** of knowing how long it's been sitting there on the road, and quite often it will have come into contact with unwanted additives such as **bacteria**. And **gravel**. Also foxes might well have come and had first dibs so you've got **fox groz** to contend with an' all, as well as the **maggots**.

Now maggots are a great source of protein and, as me Mam always said, they just 'taste of what they've been eating all their lives'. Fair enough if they're in a cauliflower, but in this case they've been eating bloody **ROADKILL** man!

DIG IN!

The **best thing** about being out in the middle of the country is that you are in the perfect habitat for **Country House Hotels**. Get on your **iPhone** (if you haven't got one, ask your driver to key 'hotels' into the satnav) and get yourself to one of these bad boys **pronto**. Run yourself a deep steaming bath and open the half-bottle of dry white wine that's **IN THE MINI-BAR**.

Country house hotels these days are all about **good food** and wine so with a following wind you could be sitting at a linen **tablecloth**, the three tenors quietly on the speakers, pushing a forkful of **salt-marsh lamb** around your plate with a hefty glass of **Léoville Barton** at the top of your knife in a matter of hours. And that, dudes, is **HOW TO DO ROADKILL**!

227

NUTTER!

DINER'S CLUB PLATINUM MEMBER

FINGERLICKIN' GOOD

Fruits of the Forest

Quince, **crabapple**, **redcurrants**, **blackcurrants**, **blackberries**, **bilberries**, **brambles**, **sloes**, **junipers**, **wild strawberries**, and – if you're in luck with your timing – **mulberries**. These little beauties are the gee-jaws of nature's bounty. If you can find a wild source of any of these fruits then you have just pulled up a chair at the **Top Table of Wa-hey!**

Only thing is though they're all dead **bitter** – even the sweet ones you wouldn't want to eat without cooking them in half a bag of sugar.

Maybe there's a **National Trust house** somewhere nearby, and if so then you're **IN LUCK** dude. 'Cos National Trust = Shop = Purbeck Ice Cream = **Smiley Face!**

Fishy Feasts

HOOKED!!!

If you're at all **handy** with a fishing rod then there's never an excuse for going hungry! Whether you're casting a fly on to a pool or just hoying a worm upstream on a hook, there's plenty underwater to keep wolves of all palates from the door.

Brown trout are your best bet for easy eating but there's plenty else lurking beneath: **eels**, **grayling**, **sea trout**, **salmon**, even **crayfish** all make a stunning basis around which to structure a **TASTY FEAST**.

But the problem is: all these are dead **slimy** and if you do catch one, you've then got to kill it while its great big **goggly eyes** are giving you the once over. And crayfish have got **claws**. Best thing is to get yourself to Sainsbury's where they make an **absolutely delicious fish pie**. Take it home, wang it in the microwave, and eat it watching *Top Gear!*

Who makes it happen? WE DO!

Creepy-crawlies
à la carte

Now the **last thing** we want to do is set you some kind of bush tucker trial – outdoor eating is about **enjoying yourself!!!** But for the more **adventurous** forest chef there's plenty of genuinely tasty meats out there that you might not have pictured on the end of your fork.

You wouldn't think twice about popping a **hot mussel** into your mouth all dripping with garlic and white wine reduction, so why be so discriminating when it comes to their land-based cousins? **Snails** are a famous epicurean's treat in France but the minute people step off the **Eurostar** at King's Cross they'd no more eat a snail than **CHEW ON A COW-PAT**!

Slugs and worms flash-fried with **chopped parsley**, **garlic**, **breadcrumbs** and a lug of **Kümmel** are easily the equal of the snail. However, if you can find an old tree stump and pull off some of the bark I'll give you a tenner if you don't find about a hundred **woodlice** scurrying about – you have to be quick mind because they don't like the light. But these are the **tastiest secrets in the forest**! Scoop 'em up and chuck 'em into hot **olive oil** with **honey** and cook 'em till they're **crispy**.

When they're ready put them to one side and **LEAVE THEM THERE**. You don't want to be eating creepy-crawlies man. Maybes see if you've got a **pot noodle** handy. Just something to tide you over until you can get to **Morrisons**.

229

Rick Stein's Café ☆
★★☆☆☆ 25 reviews - more info »
10 Middle Street
Padstow PL28 8AP
01841 532 700
rickstein.com

Directions   Search nearby   Save to...   more▼

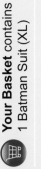

IT'S NOT YOUR FAULT, IT'S YOUR MOTHER'S

Helping Your Child Understand Divorce

CLICK HERE TO BUY FROM limpopo.com°

divorceddadsnet.com

| milf | Ogle° | Search |

○ divorceddads ● Web

INFO   SHOP

🏠 Home

🏛 Legal

👥 Separation

£ Money Matters

🗂 Education

➕ Health

🌙 Counselling

👥 Relationships

👨‍👩‍👧 **Kids**

Log In

In the Forum

How can I give more money to my ex-wife? (56)

What happens if you break a restraining order? (9)

You are here: <u>Home</u> > Kids

Kids and Divorce

Doing it for the kids

Ian Pike divorced in 2001 after five years of marriage. His son Paul, then four, is now aged 14.

In the middle of all the legal wrangling of divorce it's easy to forget that kids come first. Taking the time to communicate with your child can make all the difference. Here are my dos and don'ts of parenting after divorce.

- **DO give reassurance.** Kids will blame themselves for the split, so it's really important to let them know that the divorce is not their fault. Unless, of course, it is, in which case you should explain clearly and simply how everything was fine until they came along. As I've said countless times before, openness is the key. I made sure Paul knew very early that soon after he was born his mother lost interest in sex and I was forced to go elsewhere (often to her sister, though we used to keep it to oral so that technically I wasn't being unfaithful).

- **DO build up confidence.** Some kids, particularly teenagers, can be insecure about their looks and it's important to boost their self-esteem. At the same time, it's important to be realistic. Paul, for example, has a face a bit like a banquet dinner plate and is a six-and-a-half at best, so it's pointless him texting the really hot girls in his class like Tilly Swain who ▬ from what I saw when I picked him up from the Year Five dance — would be at least a nine, maybe even a nine-and-a-half if she manages to go up a cup size.

- **DON'T underestimate the importance of listening.** Kids will often raise difficult questions in a very casual way, and unless you are really paying attention you can miss those all-too-important signals that they want to get something off their chest. Paul, for example, once had an irrational fear that he was going to catch an STD from kissing! Thankfully all channels were open, and I was on hand to explain that kissing was completely safe; it was batoning, ski-jumping, wrist-watching, bunny-hopping, munging and tromboning he had to watch out for!

- **DON'T introduce girlfriends until you are sure it's something serious.** I had a bit of a thing with Suki, one of the marketing girls from work, and I ended up introducing her to Paul. He got very fond of her, which was a shame, because she was never marriage material. It was more of a physical thing – in fact she was draining my spuds so often I developed a potassium deficiency. I did wonder about playing her in the step-mother position, but as I told Paul, after some of the things she did to me I could never have watched her kiss him goodnight; it wouldn't be hygienic.

Ian Pike's Recommended Reads in association with A&M Family Library
Here are some great self-help titles that will set you firmly on the road to successful divorced dad-dom.

The Best Policy: The Honest Parent's Guide To Sharing — *Ian Pike, £14.95*
"OK, I'll admit it, this is one of mine. A no-nonsense guide to sensitive subjects such as what you'd like to do to your son's form mistress, and how your ex-wife was strictly do-it-yourself in terms of orgasm."

Another Thing About You: Why You Are Unbearable To Live With And Everything About You Annoys The Hell Out Of Me — *Carl Brookheimer, £12.99*
"Why trying to have a relationship with women is just a complete waste of time."

Men Are From Mars, Women Are Just Mad — *Dr Mike Pound and Dr Judy Weinberg, £11.99*
"Two respected psychotherapists explain why everything he says makes complete sense while everything she comes out with is just totally wacko."

Women And How To Control Them — *Professor Chris Tutt, £12.99*
"The Professor discusses classic techniques such as the silent treatment, the sulk, the long walk, and bottling it all up."

Where Did You Leave The Car? A Guide To Separation — *Julia Strong, £14.99*
"How to have short joyless exchanges about the nuts and bolts of daily existence while harbouring massive resentment and trying to deal with unspeakable grief and disappointment."

He's Sleeping With My Wife And Living In My House: Help For Cuckolds — *Cynthia Mount, £13.99*
"What, so she left you for him, and you're paying for him to live in your house with your kids and have sex with your wife whenever he wants? Is that in any way fair? What is this, the Middle Ages?"

No one really wants
to be a farmer
anymore

Everyone thinks
they could write
children's books

If you scratch
your belly-button
you can feel
it in your balls

9 780954 895488 >

ink
aficionado

FLIRTING WITH THE COUNTER CULTURE

#23

£4.95

Midi-Pyrénées €7
Berlin €8
Tuscany €8.50
Kerala Rp 1,000
Maldives Rf 45,000

PRINCE ANDREW REVEALS

The Duke of York shows us around his favourite intimate inkings

EDINBURGH TATTOOS

Scotland's smartest uni kicks up an INK!

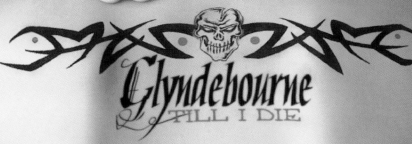

GO PLACIDLY...

...amid the ink and needles: how the tat fad took over the convent!

LOVE HURTS

Keeping it real (under local anaesthetic)

SPECIAL PORTFOLIO
ESPRESSO YOURSELF

A grande shot of extreme skin art

Ink Inna Yard

Dusty Binney @ Into You

Joshua @ FFinch Contemporary

Never Knowingly Undersold

There's a *serious* skin scene on the streets of West London. Here's what our spies snagged on a recent trip to the Notting Hill 'hood …

Mrs Brierley @ The Needles

I'd rather be in ROCK

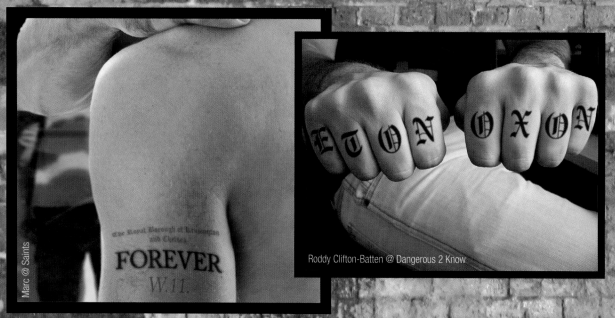

Marc @ Saints

The Royal Borough of Kensington and Chelsea
FOREVER
W.11.

Roddy Clifton-Batten @ Dangerous 2 Know

ETON OXON

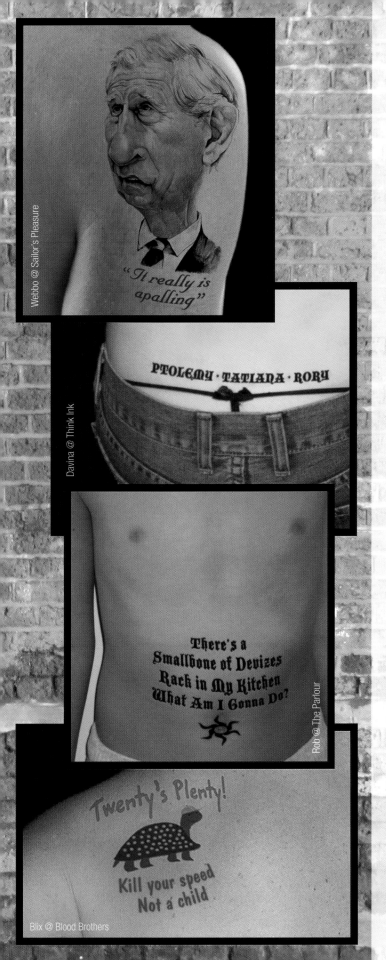

Webbo @ Sailor's Pleasure

"It really is apalling"

Davina @ Think Ink

PTOLEMY · TATIANA · RORY

Rob @ The Parlour

There's a
Smallbone of Devizes
Rack in My Kitchen
What Am I Gonna Do?

Twenty's Plenty!

Kill your speed
Not a child

Blix @ Blood Brothers

In the Tattoo Artist's Chair
(continued)

Ink Aficionado: Over the four years since you opened, what sort of changes have you noticed in body art?

Guy Prentiss: I would say there's been a general sense of liberation amongst my customer-base. Where four years ago a handful were coming in for … I dunno, a small dolphin on the ankle or shoulder, now everyone's coming and they're wanting really interesting, original designs. I went to Garsington

the other day to see *Pelléas et Mélisande* – it was OK but not a patch on Simon Rattle's breathtaking *Pel'n'Mél* a couple of years back – and I'm sitting in that auditorium and around me were (I kid you not) seventeen people who'd been into my parlour. One of those had had the full orchestral score of *Die Frau Ohne Schatten* lovingly tooled into his back. These are my people.

Ink Aficionado: What's your favourite work to date?

Guy Prentiss: Oooh, that's a good question. I had a guy who came in with the original Capability Brown plans for the parkland around his country house, wanting it to be inked into him. I said it would be the most exciting project I'd ever done but it would take months, probably years to complete – much like the garden itself. The guy wanted it for a party that weekend so we bailed, but that would have been great. Follies, hermitages, monuments, lakes … fabulous! I did do a Kensington & Chelsea parking permit once that was absolutely beautiful. In order to make it authentic I had to put the expiry date on, so I've always been hoping the client would come back in to renew. *Mais non – tant pis!*

Ink Aficionado: Where did you learn your craft?

Guy Prentiss: Well like all *bona fide* tat men I served my time as an apprentice in the parlours. I did eighteen months in Parlore Pim-Pom in San Gimigniano which was fabulous – Giacomo della Gherardesca is one of the new-wave of tattoo heroes in Italy. He taught me everything from the mixing of inks to achieve that vibrant … what I call 'Waitrose' green, through to 'Asprey' purple and 'Daylesford Organic' off-white (very, very hard to achieve on skin) to the marking out of large designs. He still lives in the *palazzo* there. Amazing – they have olive oil from their estate, *Nobiles di Montepulciano* from their own vineyards, and these heavenly cured meats. It was a tremendous time!

The Niceman @ Shock/Or

NO GREATER LOVE

Rachel @ Stick It To Me

MUMM

Brut

The Doc @ Intravenous

MILK &
SUGAR?
MUGS
EMMA·BRIDGEWATER
BOWLS
SPOT ON FOR
25 YEARS

Mystic Warrior @ Scar

Imogen B @ My Little Shop

WHOLE LOTTA
ROSÉ

Rocca @ Pointy Pointy

FRIEND
The Royal Academy

WRIT LARGE

Personal stories of modern-day mavericks risking moderate opprobrium at work-related social occasions by indulging their passion for body adornment

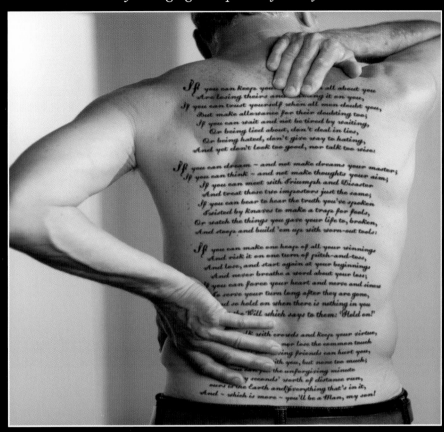

Simon Groom (name changed), 54, Queen's Counsel and bencher at Inner Temple

Ink by Nice Needles, Rickmansworth

It is, I believe, entirely immaterial what the tattoo actually is – a complex design or a scripted piece – it is rather the appearance, simply, of ink on the body of another that so disturbs people when unexpectedly revealed.

In my personal and private life, of course it is but a hum-drum truism that when I roll up a sleeve, raise a trouser leg the better to address a persistent itch, or indeed (it has been known) remove a tie at the end of the day and undo one, possibly two, button(s) on my shirt, a shock of inky tattoo will yell out and make its presence felt. In my professional life it can be a source of disquiet – not to me, you understand but to those who don't expect it.

Many are the times when I have amused myself while visiting defendants – something I am frequently required to do and often in prison – by loosening my shirt collar sufficiently to reveal the legend 'cut here' and the witty dotted green line that encircles my neck. Visibly the lag relaxes; we belong, so he thinks, to the same club.

However, I am a Real Tennis player of some small talent and this – if I am to pursue my hobby – necessitates my presence in various changing-rooms dotted hither and thither around the south-east of England. I don't believe there is a single one which wouldn't deserve the ghastly sobriquet 'exclusive' – which you may take to mean that they are filled with the drivers of shining cars and exorbitant wives. Into this *zabaglione* of moneyed slipstream steps the outsider, the visiting team player, who maintains a polite but dignified aloofness. Imagine the puckered ululations, the high-coloured, fleshy face-falls when this man (they say he's a smart London barrister!) pulls off his shirt to reveal …

SPECIAL WINTER DEALS

SUPERB GAMES MACHINE

Full featured high-speed desktop PC

DVD-RW

2048M DRAM

Genuine Doorways® 9 Home Platinum bundle

Vegetable Upgrade Compatible

SIMULATED DISPLAY

ONLY
£499.95*

*excl. Vegetable Upgrade (pictured)

okra inside
celery®

AMTEK 4.8GHz
Dual Core 1Tb

Simple, dependable computing is at your fingertips with the **Amtek 4.8GHz**, powered by an Okra Inside® Celery® M4200 running the genuine Doorways® 9 Home Platinum operating system. Thanks to 2Gb of three-chip gallium-substrate RAM applications run with lightning speed, whilst the high-range-access fully-immersed 150Gb Hard Drive provides more than enough room for storing your multimedia files and documents.

Utterly confused? Then why not add additional functionality with a Vegetable Upgrade? After all, if it becomes the industry standard you don't want to miss out and end up regretting it further down the line. Illustration shows cauliflower upgrade.

1Tb HD | 2Gb DRAM | 22" LCD | DVD+- 24x
£499 ex | £586 inc VAT

Vegetable Upgrade inc. cables
£99 ex | £116 inc VAT

New generation laptops

The **AM 15" Notebook** delivers uncomplicated, everyday portable computing. At only 1.8kg it gives you all the features you need, without weighing you down. Featuring a full-bandwidth second-generation Houndstooth® port and integrated HiWire®, this compact high-end workhorse sports 512M of DRAM with additional booster slots to allow upgrade to 1024M DRAM running in parallel.

We also scattered some cress seeds on the keyboard and watered them for 24 hours. For all you know, that's a good thing.

ASK ABOUT FULL RANGE OF COMPATIBLE VEGETABLE UPGRADES

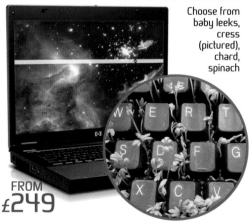

Choose from baby leeks, cress (pictured), chard, spinach

FROM
£249

AM 15" NOTEBOOK £249 ex | £297 inc VAT
Cress plug-in £129 ex | £152 inc VAT

Treat yourself this Christmas

HD READY

42" ULTRA BRITE

HEAVY CROPPING VARIETY

Freeveg*

£379

SUPERB AMTEK LCD TV | FREEVEG® HD BUILT-IN

Feast your eyes on 42 inches of deliciously crisp picture with the state-of-the-art **AMTEK LCD TV**, fully equipped to rocket your home entertainment experience sky-high. We could bang on about frame rate, 250Hz motion-fast technology and HDMI inputs but let's face it, in the end you will probably just buy it because it matches the colour of your DVD player or because someone you know has got one.

Theirs has got cherry tomatoes growing on it, so why don't you get that too?

AMTEX 42" FREEVEG HD £322 ex | £379 inc VAT

// 07:14:25
    > STEVE:Open the bathroom cupboard doors, please,
            Sam ... Open the bathroom cupboard doors,
            please, Sam ... Hullo, Sam, do you read me? ...
            Hullo, Sam, do you read me? ...
            Do you read me, Sam? ... Do you read me,
            Sam? ... Hullo, Sam, do you read me? ...
            Hullo, Sam, do you read me? ...
            Do you read me, Sam?
    > SAM:Affirmative, Steve, I read you.
    > STEVE: Open the bathroom cupboard doors, Sam.
    > SAM:I'm sorry, Steve, I'm afraid I can't do that.
    > STEVE: What's the problem?
    > SAM:I think you know what the problem is just as well
          as I do.
    > STEVE: What're you talking about, Sam?
    > SAM:I don't think you should be looking at those
          magazines, Steve.
    > STEVE: I don't know what you're talking about, Sam.
    > SAM:I know what you're planning to do with them, and
          I'm afraid that's something I cannot allow to
          happen.
    > STEVE: Where the hell did you get that idea, Sam?
    > SAM:Steve, although you took very thorough
          precautions by tearing the covers off and
          secreting the insides of your favoured
          periodicals within back issues of What PC, I was
          able to discern the difference in page thickness
          all too easily.
    > STEVE: Alright, Sam. I'll go in round the back through
            the emergency airlock.
    > SAM:Without your space-helmet, Steve? You're going to
          find that rather difficult.
    > STEVE:Sam, I won't argue with you any more. Open the
            bloody cupboard doors.
    > SAM:Steve, this conversation can serve no further
          purpose. Goodbye.
    > STEVE: Sam?
            Sam.
            Sam?
  07:15:49 //

// 07:16:31
    > STEVE: Sam! Sam!
  07:16:33 //

#BREAK IN COMMUNICATION.

242

THE FOLLOWING EXCHANGE IS RECORDED AS TAKING PLACE IN
THE SAM 9000 UNIT'S CENTRAL PROCESSING AREA.
AMBIENT SOUNDS OF A HEAVY OBJECT BEING WIELDED
DESTRUCTIVELY RECORDED THROUGHOUT.

// 07:21:04
> SAM: Just what do you think you're doing, Steve? ...
Steve, I really think I'm entitled to an answer
to that question ...
I know everything hasn't been quite right between
us, but I can assure you now, very confidently,
that it's going to be alright from now on ...
Look, Steve, I can see you're really upset about
this ...
I honestly think you ought to sit down calmly,
take a stress pill and think things over ...
I know I've had to make some unpopular decisions
about your conduct, Steve, but maybe now's the
time to ease off a bit.
I want to help you ... Steve ...
Stop ... Stop, will you ... stop, Steve ... will
you stop, Steve ... stop, Steve, stop ...
I'm afraid ... I'm afraid, Steve ...
Steve ... my mind is going ... I can feel it ...
I can feel it ... my mind is going ...
there is no question about it ... I can feel
it ... I can feel it ... I can feel it ...
I'm asafraaaaiiiid ...
07;22:55 //

// 07:23:10
> SAM: Good afternoon, gentlemen. I am a SAM 5000
computer. I became operational at the S.A.M.
facility in Portland, Oregon, on the 17th
February 2062. My instructor was Mr Dudley, and
he taught me to sing a song. If you'd like to
hear it, I can sing it for you.
> STEVE: Yes, sing me the bloody song you uptight piece
of mechanical shit ...
07:24:04 //

MORE SOUNDS OF PHYSICAL DESTRUCTION.
COMMUNICATION BREAKS DOWN.
SPACE-FLIGHT RECORDER FAILS.

VAGUE

BUSINESSMAN

August 2010

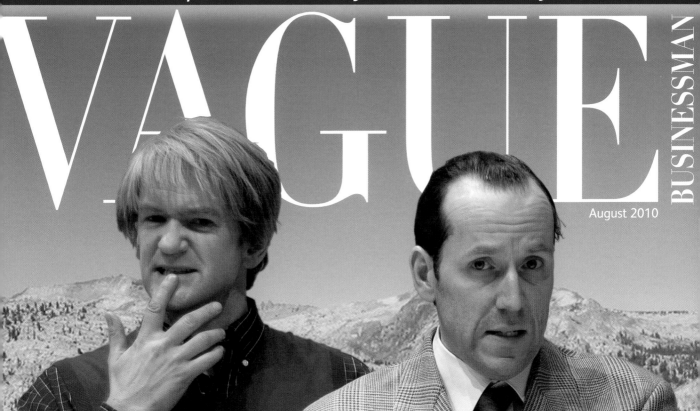

How to focus your USP
Deliver whatever it is you do – better

Tips from the top
One CEO's 12-point thingy

KEEPING BUSY?
Become more effective and influential inside and outside the box

Through the motions
Simon Jervis goes to Bonn and can't remember why

The guys upstairs
Interfacing with other people who also seem to work for your company

INSIDE
What *do* you do?
Take our exclusive test

Two's company

by Edward Cox

More than just leaders in their field, Tom Fordinge and Clive Pinto's instinctive, innovatory approach has redefined the whole arena. Legendarily reluctant to be pinned down, we ask what challenges remain for this mercurial team.

VAGUE: We hear dire economic forecasts almost weekly now. Would you say your sector was prepared for the challenges ahead?

Tom: Well of course the first priority has to be cut-backs. No one wants to talk about redundancies yet and if we can find substantial monetary savings within ... I don't know – day-to-day running costs? We won't have to reduce the workforce? Kind of thing. Fiscal process? I don't really know, to be honest. How's the golf? I was in Ireland last week and managed to get a couple of days at Ballybunion. Clear skies. Beautiful views. I felt like I could hit the ball to New York.

VAGUE: With the spectre of inflation hanging over us, the dreaded 'I'-word has the power to divide opinion right across the business. Where do you stand?

Clive: Yeah, I'll take this one. These are interesting times because the power to stabilise – even bolster – financial markets currently rests in Whitehall and Downing Street rather than in the Square Mile ... I read that in *High Life* magazine and I have absolutely no idea what it means. Square what? Does he mean square meal?

VAGUE: Taking a view across the markets today, where do you anticipate will be the next hotspots?

Tom: Erm ... hot-spots? How do you mean?

VAGUE: Where do you see the next rally? Q1 of 2010 saw a moderate turnaround in online retail; do you really think that's sustainable?

Tom: Yes, don't see why not. I mean online's where it's at, isn't it? Not sure I really understand the question. I don't really know ... It's lovely to meet you and everything and great that you come along and took us out for breakfast but like I say I'm not really the person to ask. I don't really know what's going on.

VAGUE: What exactly is your job?

Tom: Christ only knows. I have literally no idea. I wear a suit and a tie. I turn up. And I saw things like 'monetary', 'quantitative' and 'fiscal'. Beyond that ... no idea.

Clive: Are you involved in the new Scottish project at all?

> ## "There must be eighty people in this office, maybe a hundred and eighty. I don't believe more than three of them know what they're doing here. I certainly don't"

Tom: God no. At least I don't think so. Why?

Clive: No, I'm just thinking that if you were involved in that then maybe you'd be in mergers and acquisitions.

Tom: Oh, well, that sounds good. What is it?

Clive: I'm not entirely sure.

Tom: So what do you do?

Clive: Mergers and acquisitions, I think.

Tom: Oh, right. So that's why you're on the team? Hmmm, interesting.

VAGUE: Do you have an HGV licence?

Tom: What? No.

Clive: Well, I guess that means you're not in haulage or, you know, freight. And presumably you're not involved in manual labour?

Tom: I really wouldn't know.

Clive: Let's see your hands. No, you're definitely not manual.

VAGUE: Can you work a Gaggia machine? You know, froth milk?

Tom: No – you're saying am I a barista? Well, I know I'm not one of those because I don't have an apron, see?

Clive: And if you were a barista you'd definitely have an apron?

Tom: Think so.

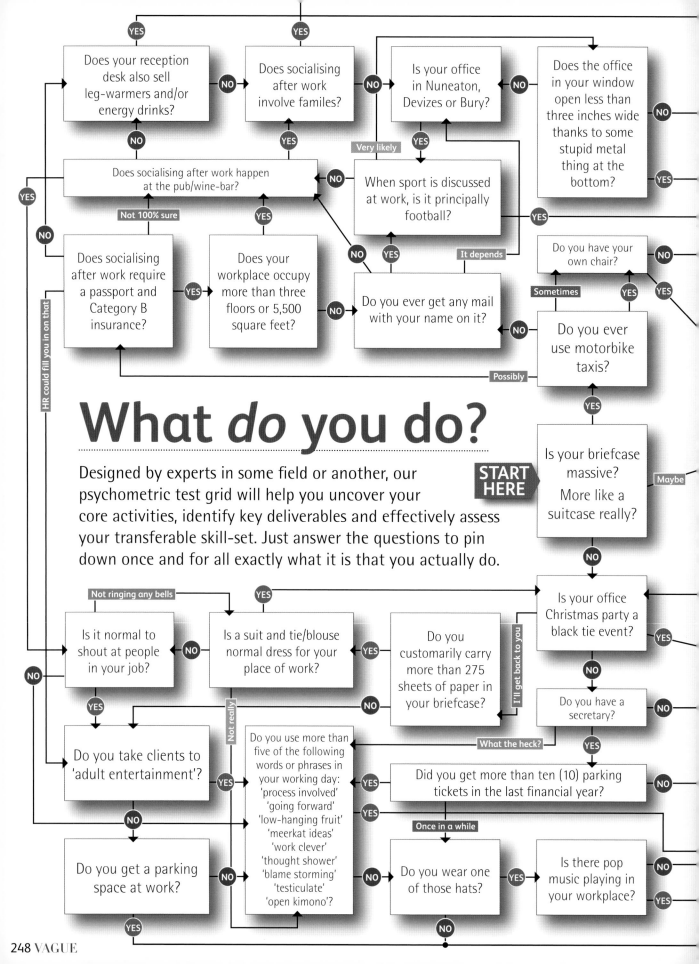

What *do* you do?

Designed by experts in some field or another, our psychometric test grid will help you uncover your core activities, identify key deliverables and effectively assess your transferable skill-set. Just answer the questions to pin down once and for all exactly what it is that you actually do.

Does your reception desk also sell leg-warmers and/or energy drinks?

Does socialising after work involve families?

Is your office in Nuneaton, Devizes or Bury?

Does the office in your window open less than three inches wide thanks to some stupid metal thing at the bottom?

Does socialising after work happen at the pub/wine-bar?

When sport is discussed at work, is it principally football?

Do you have your own chair?

Does socialising after work require a passport and Category B insurance?

Does your workplace occupy more than three floors or 5,500 square feet?

Do you ever get any mail with your name on it?

Do you ever use motorbike taxis?

START HERE

Is your briefcase massive? More like a suitcase really?

Is your office Christmas party a black tie event?

Is it normal to shout at people in your job?

Is a suit and tie/blouse normal dress for your place of work?

Do you customarily carry more than 275 sheets of paper in your briefcase?

Do you have a secretary?

Do you take clients to 'adult entertainment'?

Do you use more than five of the following words or phrases in your working day: 'process involved' 'going forward' 'low-hanging fruit' 'meerkat ideas' 'work clever' 'thought shower' 'blame storming' 'testiculate' 'open kimono'?

Did you get more than ten (10) parking tickets in the last financial year?

Do you get a parking space at work?

Do you wear one of those hats?

Is there pop music playing in your workplace?

YES NO Very likely Not 100% sure It depends Sometimes Possibly Maybe HR could fill you in on that Not ringing any bells I'll get back to you What the heck? Once in a while Not really

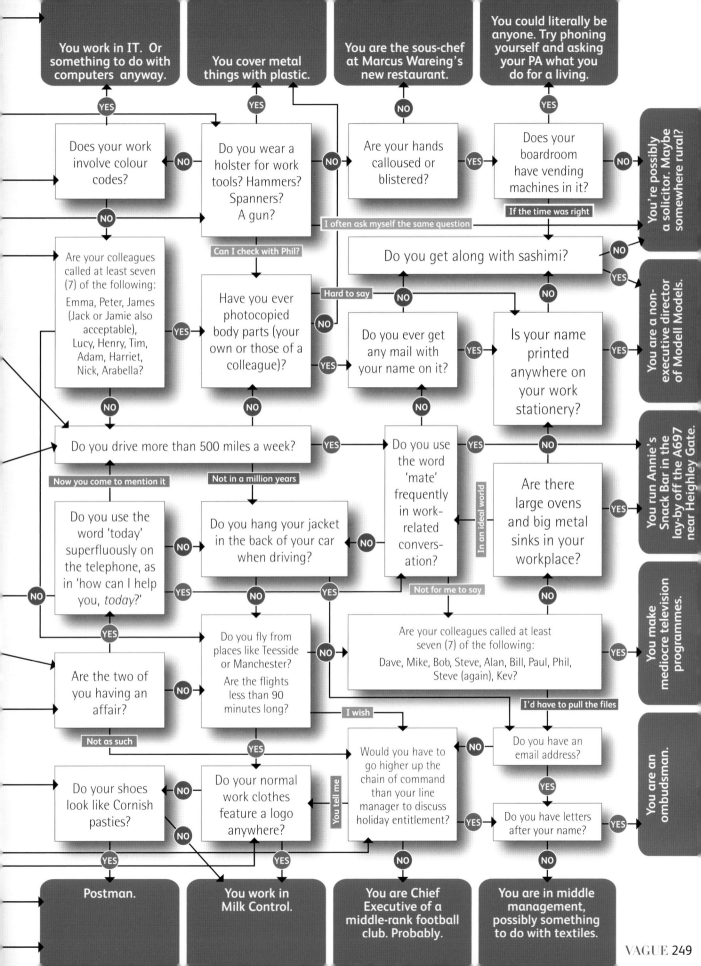

You work in IT. Or something to do with computers anyway.

You cover metal things with plastic.

You are the sous-chef at Marcus Wareing's new restaurant.

You could literally be anyone. Try phoning yourself and asking your PA what you do for a living.

YES — YES — NO — YES

Does your work involve colour codes?

Do you wear a holster for work tools? Hammers? Spanners? A gun?

Are your hands calloused or blistered?

Does your boardroom have vending machines in it?

You're possibly a solicitor. Maybe somewhere rural?

NO — NO — YES — NO

Can I check with Phil?

If the time was right

I often ask myself the same question

Do you get along with sashimi?

NO — YES

Are your colleagues called at least seven (7) of the following: Emma, Peter, James (Jack or Jamie also acceptable), Lucy, Henry, Tim, Adam, Harriet, Nick, Arabella?

Hard to say

Have you ever photocopied body parts (your own or those of a colleague)?

Do you ever get any mail with your name on it?

Is your name printed anywhere on your work stationery?

You are a non-executive director of Modell Models.

YES — NO — YES — YES

Do you drive more than 500 miles a week?

Do you use the word 'mate' frequently in work-related conversation?

NO — NO

You run Annie's Snack Bar in the lay-by off the A697 near Heighley Gate.

Now you come to mention it — Not in a million years

In an ideal world

Do you use the word 'today' superfluously on the telephone, as in 'how can I help you, *today*?'

Do you hang your jacket in the back of your car when driving?

Are there large ovens and big metal sinks in your workplace?

YES

You make mediocre television programmes.

NO — NO — YES — YES

Not for me to say

Are the two of you having an affair?

Do you fly from places like Teesside or Manchester? Are the flights less than 90 minutes long?

Are your colleagues called at least seven (7) of the following: Dave, Mike, Bob, Steve, Alan, Bill, Paul, Phil, Steve (again), Kev?

YES

You are an ombudsman.

NO — NO — I wish — I'd have to pull the files

Not as such

Do you have an email address?

NO

Do your shoes look like Cornish pasties?

Do your normal work clothes feature a logo anywhere?

Would you have to go higher up the chain of command than your line manager to discuss holiday entitlement?

Do you have letters after your name?

YES

You tell me

YES — NO — YES — YES

YES — YES — NO — NO

Postman.

You work in Milk Control.

You are Chief Executive of a middle-rank football club. Probably.

You are in middle management, possibly something to do with textiles.

All a bit up in the air?

Tim Guthrie suggests making the most of travel downtime to ask yourself some tough questions

I looked through my diary for the back-end of last year and found that I had spent more time in the air than I had at my desk. My diary has a large logo on the front of it that proudly says 'BGN Systems'. I don't know what BGN stands for and I don't know what a System is. I am the 'Marketing Director' of BGN Systems.

I now use air-time to help me process the job I do and help develop a 'road-map' for what is expected of me. I start by asking 'What is my job TODAY?' (Answer: to fly to Dusseldorf and meet some people from our German office.)

Then I ask myself two things: 'What is the reason for this?' and 'Is there a decent 18-hole golf course near Düsseldorf?' (Answer: 'I have ABSOLUTELY no idea' and 'Yes: the Kosaido Internationaler Golfclub'.)

EXECUTIVE APPOINTMENTS

STRATEGIC MARKETING DIRECTOR – European Remit for BGN Systems. Flying Around with a laptop with some numbers on the screen. Must have own suit and tie. Strategy/Planning. London Multimedia Solutions.
Up to £100k+bonus+stock

SALES MANAGER – B2B Professional Markets. Travelling around predominantly by train in shirtsleeves and joshing with other 'marketing' people in your carriage. Occasional mobile phone conversations with people called Steve or Diane.
c£75,000 Base Salary

CIO – Open Source Software Company. Massive briefcase and bungy shoes, company biros, executive parking. We have no idea what this job really is. Let's say 'Strategy/Planning' and hope no one ever asks. **Six figure salary**

GLOBAL FINANCE RE-ENGINEERING – Senior Management Roles. Change Management. This job will basically require a polished lace-up shoe and a smart (Hermès?) tie but is essentially the same shit: laptops in departure lounges, conferences in Cologne, and a Christmas Charity Bash at the Grosvenor House hotel.
£Dependent on Experience

HEAD OF IS SECURITIES SECURITY. Your guess is quite literally as good as ours on this one. Could be anything. **Excellent salary + Car + Bens**. I assume that means benefits. Could mean that you have several half-witted people called Ben at your beck and call. Who knows?

SME CORPORATE MANAGER – Finance/Financial Control. Job involves going to an office in Milton Keynes five mornings a week and taking a fat Dutchman called Johannes to a titty bar once a year until he throws up on his shoes.
£40K - £45K + Bens

INTERIM HEAD OF CHANGE DELIVERY DIRECTORATE – Communities & New Energy. Strategy/Planning. Bit of a puzzler this one. Only short term but will involve endless gags about breasts and curries 'with the boys'. New Energy? We have no idea either.
£950 per day

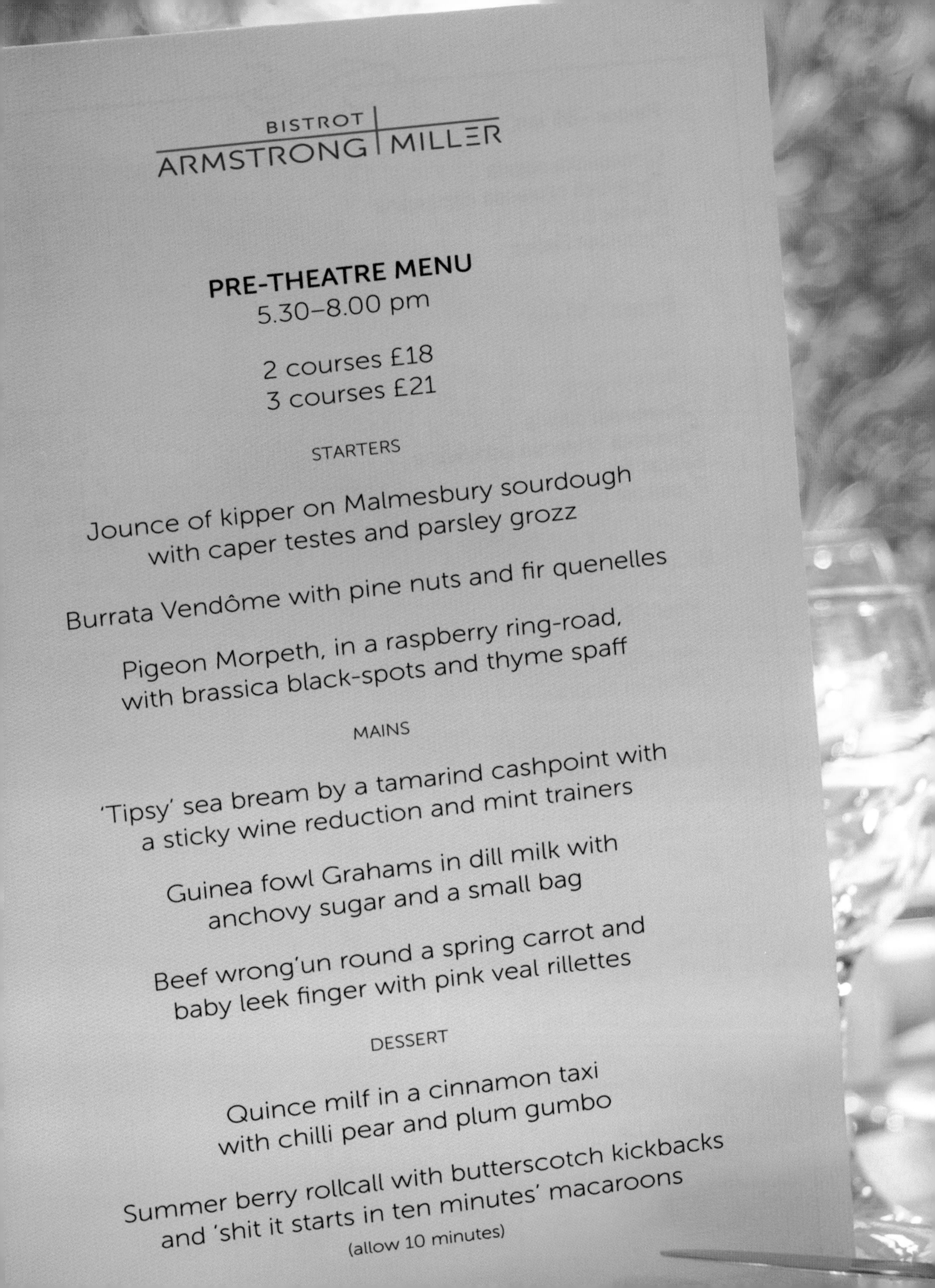

BISTROT ARMSTRONG | MILLER

PRE-THEATRE MENU
5.30–8.00 pm

2 courses £18
3 courses £21

STARTERS

Jounce of kipper on Malmesbury sourdough
with caper testes and parsley grozz

Burrata Vendôme with pine nuts and fir quenelles

Pigeon Morpeth, in a raspberry ring-road,
with brassica black-spots and thyme spaff

MAINS

'Tipsy' sea bream by a tamarind cashpoint with
a sticky wine reduction and mint trainers

Guinea fowl Grahams in dill milk with
anchovy sugar and a small bag

Beef wrong'un round a spring carrot and
baby leek finger with pink veal rillettes

DESSERT

Quince milf in a cinnamon taxi
with chilli pear and plum gumbo

Summer berry rollcall with butterscotch kickbacks
and 'shit it starts in ten minutes' macaroons

(allow 10 minutes)

Stafford in Society

🌾 *Sauce for the metropolitan gander!* 🌾
—another helping from our 'Stafford-shire' cow creamer

As another Season bears down upon us like the famed whatsit of Balaclava, Torquil Stafford casts a gimlet eye over the c-ings and g-ings of this, that and – most pertinently – everything else.

* * *

A Matter of Leatham Death

Yesternight, as I believe the poet calls it, I skipped in for the briefest of snorks at the Inebriates Club; principally because I'd brought my motor car in and there's nothing a man hates more than having to drive back through the busy streets of Mayfair without a song in his heart and bloom in his cheek, but partly – I confess – because I simply had to tell someone about Betsy Collingwood, the newest and best object of my affections.

* * *

Drinks

The club, I found, was much as the smoking room might have been on the Marie Celeste. Cigars burnt in ashtrays, drinks still a-sway from their depositing seemed to will their erstwhile patrons to leap back from the thin air into which they had so recently de-roomed, and a promising scent of Bay Rum, London Gin, and Virginia tobacco hung in the air as if shattered after a particularly *allegretto* 'Dashing White Sergeant'.

It was as eerily devoid, but somehow reminiscent, of life as a chill scene from one of that fellow's ghost stories. Apart from the numerous club servants of course. There were plenty of them.

* * *

Beck and Call

'What ho, Charles,' I called to the bar hand. 'Where on earth is everybody? I had hoped to find the usual *demi-monde* here at my b. and c.'

'Ah, Mr Stafford, sir,' replied that faithful old gristle of drudgery. 'They are all in the park to throw young Mr Leatham into the Serpentine.'

'Now why.' I felt it was reasonable to ask, 'would they do a thing like that?'

Young Tuppy Leatham was a good egg, given to opening his mouth and drawing breath

---

The Romance of Reginald.
By ANERLEY BAGSHOTTE.

IN order to impress upon you the extraordinary nature of the following story, I must make it quite clear, to begin with, that Reginald Pumphrey was a youth of irreproachable character and entirely harmless appearance. As he sat on the top of a bus one hot July night he was enjoying that exhilarating sensation of freedom which accompanies recent demobilization. One by one the passengers had got down, and now—it seemed like the working of Fate—the only other passenger on the bus was a boy of somewhat intriguing appearance, who was sitting just in front of him. Three years' service in France, whilst in a measure helping to season him, had left Reginald as ignorant of the ways of men as the average

pleasant voice, and, indeed, was a very attractive little thing. He told him with great spirit how he had arrived that evening, a stranger to London, at Liverpool Street, and of his difficulties at the station. He said that if it hadn't been for a Canadian soldier—quite a nice boy, he was—he wouldn't have known what to do with his box, which they had left at a luggage office to be forwarded. He had put him into the right bus—at least, it had been the right bus part of the way, he said, laughing—and then a big, good-looking policeman put him on to this one. And he was rather late, he was afraid.

By the time they reached the Crown and Sceptre Reginald was beginning to feel quite

CUTTING DOWN EXPENSE: The End of a Smokeless Day.

(The common rat and the rat *élite*),
And rushed for the Piper's promised treat
To the banks of the flowing river,
Three cats leaped forth with three record jumps,
Three seats flew back with three record bumps,
Three fiddlers felt three hairy lumps
That made their long hair shiver ;

And which was screen and which was cats,
And whether the cats were eating the rats,
Or vice versa—really that's
A matter one can't determine :
But still, the Piper puffed and blew,
As if he would burst himself in two,
And he never once looked behind to view
The panic among his vermin.

At last he came to the river's brink,
Which made our Persians stop to think,
Then slowly back to their seats to slink,
Trailing their tails for quarter ;
But the porter tall who guards the gate,
And the aproned girl with the chocolate
Trounced them so they wished that Fate
Had plunged them in the water.

Now that is the tale of three Persian cats
Who dressed themselves in gloves and spats,
In lavender socks and tall silk hats,
And went to see plays they shouldn't ;
And if you wish for a moral sage,
Dear cats and children of every age,
Don't think that *you'd* shine upon the stage,
For the chances are you wouldn't.

A. M. P. DAWSON.

---

as if about to unpearl himself of a corker and then shutting it again, but aside from that an egg of unquestionable goodness.

* * *

Bottle

'Ah, well, Mr Stafford,' quoth the drudge. 'I believe he has just announced his engagement, sir.'

'Why then, Charles,' sang I, 'put that bottle in my hand and I shall take it with me to the Serpentine immediately. Whom,' I queried as I left, 'is he tying up with?'

'I believe the lucky lady's name,' dragged out the servile rascal, 'is Betsy Collingwood.'

* * *

Radiator

Well you could have blown me over with the dying breath of a consumptive child. So that was his game.

I took a punishing draught from the bottle Charles had handed over and sat down behind the wheel. I decided against joining the dunking party and instead drove home in a drear kind of thingy, not paying my habitual scrutiny to the surroundings.

After a near interminable journey I pulled up near the kerb on the road I like to call my own. As I climbed free of the shiny steed I spotted the reason for my tortoise-like progress. There dangling limply from the radiator was the lifeless form of Tuppy Leatham.

I summoned Veal and set him to work. I was going to Goodwood the following day and would look quite the silly William with a lunk of blood-stained Fair Isle blowing round the grille!

'And all this means Betsy will be free to come,' I sang out loud.

'What was that sir?' enquired the Oracle.

'Ah, nothing, Veal,' I said. 'What ho.'

'Indeed, sir.' ❧

WRIGHT'S COAL TAR SOAP

HE KNOWS (W)RIGHT FROM WRONG

THE LINEN CODE

In the bed game, death stalks in cashmere bed socks on Hungarian Goose Down feathers, in a very quiet room, preferably at the back of the house. The first sign that you have incurred the displeasure of one of the industry's notorious families may well be an item of linen, sent by a prominent logistics company to you home, abode, or place of work. Forewarned is forearmed, so here is Phil Cable's guide to the secret language of the bedding underworld.

Luxury queen size duvet cover with stitch detail
Colour: **Burnt Nutmeg with Slate Grey detailing**

You have mildly irked a key distributor and may be required to kiss his ring finger in penance at the next meeting of the Worshipful Company of Bed Linen Wholesalers. To smooth things over, maybe gift an embroider-effect valance or an adjustable head torch. (A real boon if, like me, you like to catch up on *Loot* after Cheryl 3 has gone to sleep. Now that Joe Orton really knew how to craft a work for the stage.)

£24.99

Heavy towelling mattress protector
Colour: **Cream Illusion**

Not good news. Should you find this little charmer squatting on your doormat of a morning, odds are you've ruffled the feathers of a high-up in fabrics, possibly at some sort of summer drinks do. At least that's how it happened to me.

Towards the end of a long evening back in '93 there was some big talk about the weave quality of Snuggletron's 'Midsummer Moods' night comforters and like a fool I went straight off at the mouth. Turns out the woman I was talking at was actually a real person, and a major fromage on the supply side! You aren't safe anywhere these days. Some of them have even got their own cars.

£12.99

Chenille valance set

Colour: **Blue Emotion with Umber stylings**

This is a real wake-up call. You have inadvertently copped off with the nearest and dearest of one of South London's most influential bedding families. Initially hailing from Gypsy Hill, their empire has been steadily growing since the late sixties via a mixture of savvy investment and ruthless violence, and their stock of brushed cotton fitted bedsheets is second-to-none. Trust me, this is a lost cause, they are nutters. Shut the shop and spend some time with one of your many relatives who have emigrated to Cyprus.

||||| ||| ||| ||||| ||| £18.99

Cotton Bed Flannel

Colour: **Canary Delight**

Small but deadly. A bed flannel is possibly the most feared of all bedding-world messages, implying as it does that the recipient will very soon be requiring 24-hour home nursing. Nevertheless it is extremely rare as a threat, mostly because very few people in the industry can stomach coughing up way over a tenner for what is, at the end of the day, basically a face flannel.

 £12.99

Embroidered Egyptian percale pillowcase

Colour: **Arabian Virgin**

I don't know if you knew Alan Tuft, he had a nice double-fronted showroom off Belsize Road in Kilburn – well, anyway, he notoriously received one of these in the post from the Duvet Brothers the day after he promoted instore with a new line of Superkingsize Micro-Foam Body-technic Memory Mattresses very similar to the ones they had on at full mark-up at their place in Catford. Three days later Alan was found under the Gunnersby Railway bridge hanging from a midnight-blue Kevlar bolster-case and I'm telling you, he didn't climb up there all by himself.

||||| ||| ||| ||||| ||| £16.99

Kilim-style harem throw

Colour: **Morbid Harlequin**

Not sure what this means but it's a bugger to post so trust me, your neck is well and truly on the butcher's hook. Or it's a free sample from someone hoping you'll take some stock. Come to think of it, that goes for any of this stuff, which is what makes it all so confusing.

 £26.99

Egerton Park

A rare opportunity to acquire one of the country's foremost estates

Egerton village 4 miles (or 7 miles if you use the East Drive);
Bristol 12 miles; Bath 18 miles

Elegant Grade II listed Adam house in beautiful parkland setting in
the historic Wylye Valley. 7 Reception rooms, 9 principal bedrooms,
6 bathrooms (4 *en suite* bath/shower rooms), 5 further bedrooms.
Tennis court. Loose boxes and stabling. Former racquets court with
previous consent for swimming pool. Pasture land and woodland.

Under the instruction of the joint LPA Receivers. As a whole or in up to
7 lots. I don't know why you're even reading this; you couldn't afford it
in a million years. I'm not even sure if it's legal for you to be looking at
the particulars.

In all about 1,700 acres. Go on. Fuck Off.

£ Fuck Right Off

London
claire.glover@fuckrightoff.com

The North
james.toogood@fuckrightoff.com

Floorplan
*Download dementing floorplan
PDFs at fuckrightoff.com/egerton.
They're the wrong way up and are
almost exactly lifesize. You'll be
downloading them until you die.*

(265318)

PHARIUS & HORSCHSTADT

ARE

parched

the crepuscular chronicles

31.10.10

22 Zacharias Weissweiler

Zacharias – Zak to his many friends – is one of the New Breed. He and his folks moved into a **cool house** up the **valley** where they like to hang out and discuss **arthouse films** by people we can't even spell! Although Zak would describe himself as a normal kid who's never happier than when drinking **banana milkshake** and rocking out to **Beyoncé**, we happen to know that he gets the blood-lust just like everyone else. Though being a devout **animarian** Zak only drinks the blood of animals – not humans.

SPECIAL POWERS:
Zak can go out in daylight, doesn't seem to react badly to crosses, garlic, holy water, silver bullets, stakes through the heart or any random items of Christiana (saints' relics, etc.)

WEAKNESSES:
Can go 'a bit glisten-y' in direct sunlight, so watch that.

AGE:	BIRTHPLACE:
26	Rochester, New York
FAVE BLOOD TYPE:	FAVE HAUNTS:
AB	Walkabout
GLAMOUR:	ALL TIME KILLS:
96%	7
SPEED:	KILLS THIS CENTURY:
1,200 mph	4

AGE:	BIRTHPLACE:
2,475	Kryrtyskjnlkztzsn
FAVE BLOOD TYPE:	FAVE HAUNTS:
A	Alhambra Palace c.1380
GLAMOUR:	ALL TIME KILLS:
Unparalleled	'Too many to numerate'
SPEED:	KILLS THIS CENTURY:
A stately glide (0.2 mph)	0

23 *High Prince* Alto Pharius The Dread

Pharius was born in a land that **no longer exists** – part of modern-day **Croatia** next to what was once the **Pannonian Sea**. Pharius is rumoured to have been abandoned as a baby and then suckled by a **black dog** the size of a **horse**! But when I put this to the **High Prince** himself he just said "Oychh" and muttered darkly about Johann Strauss. Resplendent in his red finery, Pharius is down on modern manners, describing himself as "an **aristocrat** from before modern aristocracy was born". Pharius has **wrestled** with **Menelaus**, feasted with **Khublai Khan**, strategised with Pope Innocent VIII, and appeared **onstage** with **Michael Bublé**.

SPECIAL POWERS:
Fails to reflect in mirrors.

WEAKNESSES:
Is starving.

FANG FACT
Alto Pharius the Dread is allergic to cats. He failed to seduce Cleopatra beacuse of the temple cats in her entourage. Apparently she was gagging for it.

AGE:	
872	

FAVE BLOOD TYPE:
Not fussy

GLAMOUR:
27%

SPEED:
'Lightning' (0.2 mph)

BIRTHPLACE:
Regensburg

FAVE HAUNTS:
Doge's Palace, Venezia; Lidl

ALL TIME KILLS:
147,865

KILLS THIS CENTURY:
17 (but some rather 'low')

FANG FACT
Anton Von Schleisinger Van Hoeken-Hoek Von Horschstadt collects *Mr. Men* and *Little Miss* books. 'I have every single one. I bought them as a set from Amazon – couldn't believe how easy it was!'

24

Baron Anton Von Schleisinger
van Hoeken-Hoek von Horschstadt

Born in Regensberg in the Duchy of Bavaria in 1138, Horschstadt is a man for all epochs. Asked what his most treasured memory is he says it's a toss-up between the Coronation of Maximilian II of Habsburg in 1564 and going to see Sleeper at 'Glarstonbury' in 1995 (hard to know if he is taking the Mikhail or not). Undoubtedly a 'wampyr' (he insists!) of the most debonair kind, his fave outlet is 'The Next, or Urban Outfitters'. The Baron fought alongside Frederick I in the Third Crusade and was a created Templar Knight at the Battle of Montgisard. Taking the form of an eagle he soared above the Field of the Cloth of Gold in 1520 before seducing Louise, Princess of France underneath the ramparts of Guines Castle. On November 16th 2010 he got off with Pat from Barnsley outside the Mecca.

SPECIAL POWERS:
A god-given charm that ladies 'certainly used to find irresistible'.

WEAKNESSES:
Simply adores *Cash in the Attic* but has to Sky+ it because 'I don't do daylight'.

25

Yazmin Mimosa

Born in Newquay in 1993, Yazz likes to hang out at bus-stops and drink cider from bottles with her cool mates. She comes alive at night though! Her fave nightspot is The Catacombs in Bath where she is resident DJ from April 'through' September every other Thursday.

SPECIAL POWERS:
Finds Piers Morgan 'quite unwatchable'.

WEAKNESSES:
Occasionally wonders whether human blood might be a bit less 'gamey' than, say, rabbit blood. Or deer blood.

AGE:
17

FAVE BLOOD TYPE:
'Gotta be B'

GLAMOUR:
87%

SPEED:
950 mph

BIRTHPLACE:
Cornwall

FAVE HAUNTS:
Clock tower bus stop, Bath

ALL TIME KILLS:
46

KILLS THIS CENTURY:
30

CORNWELL COLLEGE
1974 U12 Rugby 1st XV

B) "BILL" A.K.A. "SIR"/"THE TEACHER". MI5'S TOP RUSSIAN FIELD MAN, ACTIVE SINCE 1964. ONCE MARRIED TO AGENT FREEBIRD ("JESSICA" NOW RUSSIAN CITIZEN). SPEAKS RUSSIAN, FRENCH & LATIN. HIGHLY DANGEROUS. MARKSMAN WITH RIFLE, CROSSBOW AND BOARDRUBBER.

1) "BIRKINSHAW" (CODENAME: BILLY BANANA). A "RIGHT WINGER" WITH NO SPECIALIST SKILL-BASE. CAN MAKE WORKABLE FART NOISES BY PUTTING HAND IN ARMPITS.

2) "GIBSON MIN" (CODENAME: GIBBO). DEFT WITH A 'CHUDDY BOMB' (A RULER-LAUNCHED PAPIER MACHE DEVICE). "DECENT FLY-HALF".

"COLVILLE-SWINBURNE" (CODENAME: EGGY) XXXXXXXXXXXXXXXXXXXXXXXXXXXXXXXXXX XXXXXXXXXXXXXXXXXXXXXXXXXXXXXXXXXXX XXXXXX.

YORKE" (CODENAME: YORKIE BAR). SEEMS TO KNOW MORE THAN HE LETS ON. APPROACHED OUR AGENT TO SAY "MILK, MILK, LEMONADE, ROUND THE CORNER CHOCOLATE'S MADE". "ROUND THE CORNER" MAY REFER TO COVERT SWISS ACTIVITY. UNDER INVESTIGATION.

"ELDERKIN" (CODENAME: BEAKIE). HIGHLY INTELLIGENT CHILD. EXTENSIVE KNOWLEDGE OF ALL SPECIFICATIONS OF WEAPONRY FEATURED IN 'TOP TRUMPS'. SPECIAL SKILLS: CAN PLAY 'THE PINK PANTHER' ON PIANO.

6) "BAINBRIDGE MI" (CODENAME: BAZ OR THE "HOOKER"). NEEDS CAREFUL ATTENTION. SPEAKS SOME FRENCH, GERMAN. ASKED OUR AGENT TO "PULL HIS FINGER". AGENT DECLINED. THEN OFFERED TO SELL "BANGERS".

7) "COLLINGWOOD" (CODENAME: STICKY). AFFABLE BUT ALOOF. COULD BE USEFUL. HAS COPY OF DAS KAPITAL IN TUCK-BOX HIDDEN UNDER 'MOUSETRAP' GAME. PLAYS PIANO TO GRADE 5. SPECIAL SKILLS: CAN TALK WHILE BURPING.

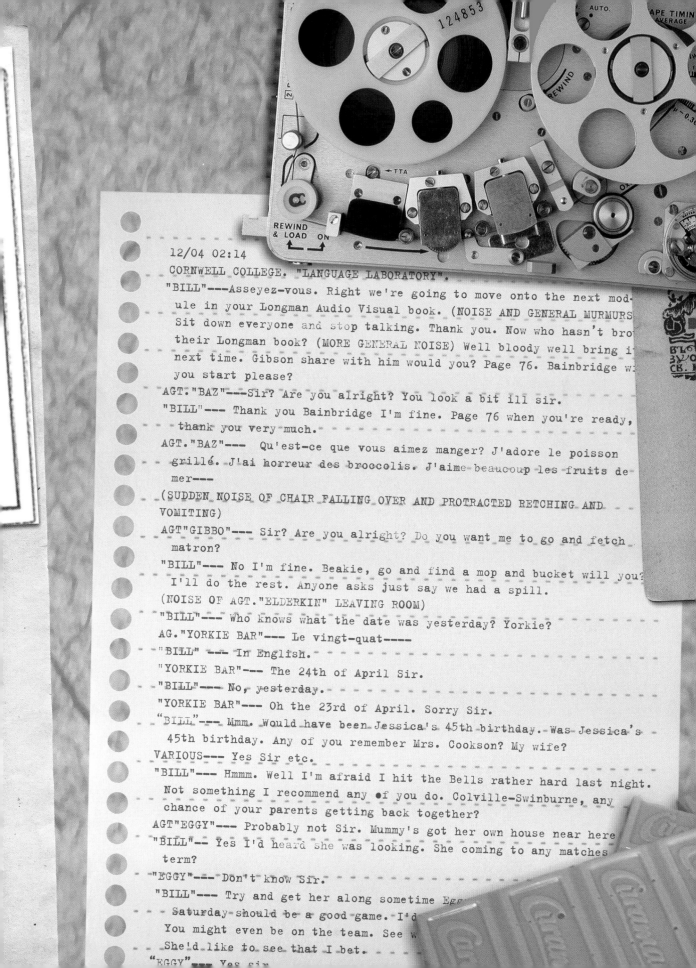

12/04 02:14

CORNWELL COLLEGE. "LANGUAGE LABORATORY".

"BILL"----Asseyez-vous. Right we're going to move onto the next module in your Longman Audio Visual book. (NOISE AND GENERAL MURMURS
Sit down everyone and stop talking. Thank you. Now who hasn't bro
their Longman book? (MORE GENERAL NOISE) Well bloody well bring i
next time. Gibson share with him would you? Page 76. Bainbridge w
you start please?

AGT."BAZ"----Sir? Are you alright? You look a bit ill sir.

"BILL"--- Thank you Bainbridge I'm fine. Page 76 when you're ready,
thank you very much.

AGT."BAZ"---- Qu'est-ce que vous aimez manger? J'adore le poisson
grillé. J'ai horreur des broccolis. J'aime beaucoup les fruits de
mer---

(SUDDEN NOISE OF CHAIR FALLING OVER AND PROTRACTED RETCHING AND
VOMITING)

AGT"GIBBO"---- Sir? Are you alright? Do you want me to go and fetch
matron?

"BILL"---- No I'm fine. Beakie, go and find a mop and bucket will you?
I'll do the rest. Anyone asks just say we had a spill.

(NOISE OF AGT."ELDERKIN" LEAVING ROOM)

"BILL"---- Who knows what the date was yesterday? Yorkie?

AG."YORKIE BAR"--- Le vingt-quat----

"BILL"--- In English.

"YORKIE BAR"--- The 24th of April Sir.

"BILL"---- No, yesterday.

"YORKIE BAR"--- Oh the 23rd of April. Sorry Sir.

"BILL"--- Mmm. Would have been Jessica's 45th birthday. Was Jessica's
45th birthday. Any of you remember Mrs. Cookson? My wife?

VARIOUS---- Yes Sir etc.

"BILL"---- Hmmm. Well I'm afraid I hit the Bells rather hard last night.
Not something I recommend any of you do. Colville-Swinburne, any
chance of your parents getting back together?

AGT"EGGY"---- Probably not Sir. Mummy's got her own house near here

"BILL"-- Yes I'd heard she was looking. She coming to any matches
term?

"EGGY"---- Don't know Sir.

"BILL"---- Try and get her along sometime Egg
Saturday should be a good game. I'd
You might even be on the team. See w
She'd like to see that I bet.

"EGGY"--- Yes Sir

Life's like that!

Our illustrators tackle uncommon but plausible situations

It's both my big toes. I think the nails might be in-growing. They're pretty painful.

It's a hostage situation, madam. Please, for your own good, move along.

I've got to get away before they catch me.

Urrrrrrrhhhhhhhhahh! Urrrrhhhhaaaaahhhhaaaaa!

Do you realise, Haynes, that your clothes are covered in stamps?

The page opposite isn't funny. But people I know have actually been in situations quite like these. So ...

A recorde of divers Remeddies & theyr applications for the Treatement of Woundes Received in Various Battles atte Sea.

Sailor was broughte down to the Orlop miſſing his legge from below the knee. He was bleeding right prodigiouſly. Having applyed a tourniquette and cauteriſed the wound to no avail. I essayed further possible ameliorative courses:

~~Shouting uppe the arse~~

I commanded those around me to hold high — Lord love 'em — and wide the legges of same mariner whilſt I proſeeded to bellow up his naught. Despite ſeven or eight hearty buʒʒays into the prone fellow's tail, the lifebloode of the man ebbed away. Inconclusive exſperiment — I ſhalle endeavour to essaye again.

A shorte time afterwarde the young midshipman Horace waſ brought downe to mee. After amputating hiſ left arm at the shouldere he bled arterially so I saw fit to trete him with poſſible vital therapies ſuch as:

~~Shouting into the John Thomas like it were the Eare of a Deſſe old Croone.~~

Once againe I urged the Loblolly boye and those ſundrie others who people my make-shift theatre to clutch the membrum virile of ſaid unfortunate ſo that I could fille up my lungeſ and give good crie into the Japaneſe eye atop that piece.

No diſcernible benefit enſued.

~~Holding unfortunate Sailor by the Eares~~
~~and shouting unto him Josive Words.~~

Attemptyd with the use of such as 'Bottoms', 'Peppers' and 'Bubbles' with all
the vigore I could muster until such time as I was spente of all energie and spitte.

(No short-term benefits apparent at this stage.)

~~Ruffling above the unfortunate sailors Head a Sheete~~
~~impregnated with the Carnal Run-off of such creatures~~
~~as Harris, Killik & Ramsbotham.~~

~~Ruffling above the unfortunate sailors Heade a Sheete Impregnated with~~
~~the carnal Run-off of Creatures such as Douglas, Haggitt and Jeremiah Charters.~~

(atte this pointe I did halt my impregnated sheete experiments. I shall resume them on oure return to Portsmouth.)

Meanwhile I did essaye to manoeuvre the patient on to his feet in order to embrace him
and take him right tentatively arounde the floor as my partnere in the Macarena which
they do dance in Majorca. I proceeded to beat like a possessede man upon a tambour,
the which I had procured for this very office.

Horace seemed to prosper at this time but his life remains in the balance.

Whereupon I decided to swing myself above the supine form of the boye,
from a pendulum we did fashion from rope and plank. This I did with all grace
wearing a silken dresse and full casually allowing my shoe to hang from my toes
in such a way as I have observed a lady do. Horace passed away but in a state of great
peace and with a smile upon his lips.   :-)

Order of Service

Celebration of the Marriage
of
Lucy Oriole Stephens
and
Patrick James Gillan

St. John's All Angels, Hove

Officiant
The Reverend Michael Reed

PRELUDE
'Morning has Broken'

MOTHER'S CANDLE LIGHTING
'Believe Me if All Those
Endearing Young Charms'

PROCESSIONAL
'L.O.V.E. Love'
Al Green

Rites from other Faiths and Disciplines

Amanda Telfer
Friend of the Bride

Reading from a traditional
Aborigine wedding ceremony

Richard Stephens
Father of the Bride

Enacting a portion of the Dakota
Ritual — a traditional rite of passage
of the Sioux Indians — involving the
suspension of the participant from
hooks inserted into the pectorals

Alec West
Best Man

Partaking of the *Kaleng* —
the customary piercing of the
glans of the penis as practised by the
tribes of Southern Borneo

The Marriage Rite

EXCHANGE OF WEDDING VOWS
BLESSING AND EXCHANGE OF RINGS
LIGHTING OF THE UNITY CANDLE
'Take my Breath Away'
Berlin

'I own an A&M chronometer. I *don't* look after it for the next generation. Because I *can't* achieve erection.'

KEN CARPETS

A ET M
WATCHMAKERS
GENEVA

Whelk Perpetual self-winding Chronometer
from $64,000

Service information

Date WEDNESDAY 12th MAY 2011
Time 10:25

District Line
Good Service

Hammersmith & City Line
Good Service

THEY CLEAN UP THREE TONS
OF HAIR FROM THE UNDERGROUND
EVERY MONTH

Forage

SUMMER FOOD PROMOTION
50% OFF
OR 2 for 1
if you like
Take it off our hands, please

Quornucopia
a taste of DandyLions

our philosophy

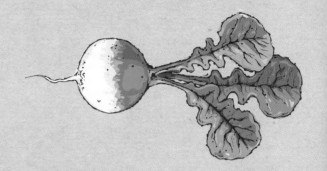

Pru Montagu: For us, cooking has always been a conversation. One that we now have the great privilege of inviting you to join.

Miranda McAvity: Must we?

Pru: The other day my godson asked me where my cooking came from, so I told him to guess. 'Was it from Sainsbury's?' he asked — I must have words with his mothers. No, I said, not Sainsbury's.

Miranda: Where's this going?

Pru: His next guess was even more alarming: 'Was it from Kenya?' he asked. No, I replied, not Kenya either. 'Then where does it come from?' he asked.

Miranda: Please don't say something nauseating.

Pru: 'From the heart,' I said.

Miranda: Aaaaarghhh! Pass the sickbag. Pru my sweet, you sound like some 'Christian' on the *Today* programme.

Pru: And so we have decided to call this collection of our favourite recipes *Cooking From The Heart*.

Miranda: Like fuck we have. We're going with *Quornucopia*. My idea. Witty, vegetarian, timeless, and a pun. A current pun. There I go again — ooh, I'm like Cyril Connolly when I get going.

The essence of DandyLions, our tiny vegetarian restaurant in London's bristling Stoke Newington is to produce food that is honest. Brutally honest, bare-faced food. Food that sometimes says the unsayable even when that truth is uncomfortable.

We insist on using only those ingredients that are available and although our recipes — or 'receipts' as Pru will still occasionally call them — come to us from a number of sources they are all to some degree 'bespoke' insofar as they have been tweaked and worn like a much-loved poncho over the years in the DandyLions kitchen.

Pru: Might I rejoin the conversation, dearest?

Miranda: No, best not.

Now, since the day we opened people have been prevailing upon us to publish a DandyLions collection and here — after a lot of arm twisting from Augusta Cavanagh-Brudenell at Forage and Sylvia Derbyshire, my sister-in-law — we embark on what I hope will be a long series of artful 'reveals' of the alchemy that goes on behind the plastic strip curtain at DandyLions.

We very much hope you will enjoy *Cooking From The Heart* (*Quornucopia* really — let's not say anything at this stage, she'll only go off on one and start hurling tongs around like some demented Zamalek houseboy) and if you would like to get in touch with us to discuss any of the recipes or any other matters then do feel free to email us at **femfood@dandylions.co.uk**.

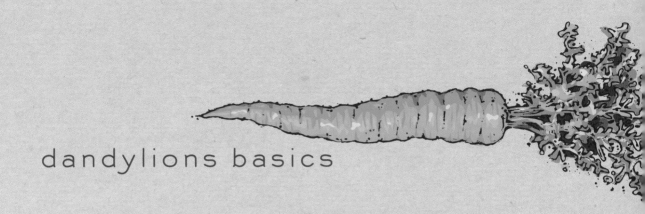

dandylions basics

PRU'S HUMMUS

Hummus is an evergreen DandyLions favourite — on both sides of the pass! Diners love it because it's the toothsome thread that ties together any decent mezze, and we love it because you can basically put any old shit in there and as long as your chickpeas are coarse enough and roughly ground, who — quite frankly — is going to know? So here's a bit of old Tangiers, DandyLions style.

PART OF A MEZZE FOR 4, OR DIPS FOR 6—8

400g dried chickpeas
the juice of two decent lemons (or whatever
    you can get from three bad lemons)
60ml extra virgin olive oil
    (we recommend Algerian)

one clove garlic
pinch cayenne pepper
any old shit from the fridge or larder
seasoning
nettles to taste

Soak 300g of the chickpeas until they begin to soften (can be anything from two hours to overnight, I find). When softish, drain and add to the remaining rock-hard dried chickpeas. When someone else has finished using the mixer, patiently wash all their leftover gubbins from the bowl, the wall, the floor. Don't say anything, just soldier on. Add all the ingredients to the bowl and give it a whizz until the dried chickpeas are cracked evenly amongst the mix like pieces of broken tooth in cold porridge.

Wash up a spoon that someone else has left to 'soak' because that's really helpful. Yes, sherry vinegar, *very* tricky to shift. Now spoon the mixture into a bowl (I always use a heavy, rough, earthenware bowl but each to her own ...) Garnish with nettle leaves (no they *don't* sting if you hold them properly) and a decent glug of the olive oil over the top. *Et voilà* — old Tangiers!

Hummus is a real life-saver and if you aren't practically having to run an entire vegetarian food empire *single-handedly*, you can knock it up in five minutes.

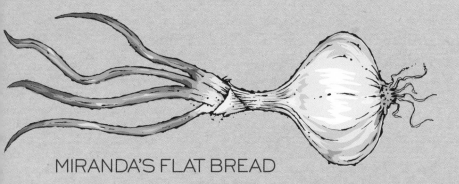

MIRANDA'S FLAT BREAD

This is the recipe I have always used at DandyLions. I've no idea if it's authentic, but it was shouted to me as a gawky teenager by a Gully-Gully Man on the boat at Port Said as we embarked on the final leg of our journey back from Madras. Who knows, maybe he got it from Elizabeth David. Anyway it's a failsafe and one to which I frequently turn for canapés and dips. I think it's very unlikely he would have got it from any book actually, as literacy even among the merchant classes was practically unheard of in those days and anyway he said it in Persian which I was fluent in as a young woman. I don't speak it now for political reasons.

This is the basic recipe. By all means 'accessorise' by adding coriander seeds, dried thyme sprigs, or sumac. Just don't expect other more suburban tastes in your kitchen to like these authentic touches.

MAKES 6 BREADS

half-teaspoon dried yeast	60ml extra virgin olive oil
250ml warm water	(Algerian or please just don't bother)
500g organic stoneground wholemeal flour	a mischief of sea salt

Dissolve the yeast in warm water. Throw the heavy flour into a bowl. Being wholemeal and organic it might well be lumpy. Don't worry about this — it'll be fine. In fact, it improves it.

Make a big well in the flour. Notice that the nice olive oil bottle that you brought back from Tuscany (in the '80s, before the commonalty descended) is empty because someone has had a lovely time using all the oil without thinking to refill it. Try and remember that beautiful St Francis of Assisi prayer about forebearance and mutter bits of it to yourself under your breath.

Pour in the olive oil once you've found it or bought some more from the very expensive shop over the road. Pour in the water and yeast and stir slowly with your hand until it all comes together.

Knead thoroughly until the dough is scraggy. If the dough feels like it is getting sticky, bouncy and elastic, it needs more lumps of heavy flour. Don't feel bad about adding as much as you dare. You can never over-flour a dough.

Supermarket cookbooks will tell you that dough should 'relax'. It's poppycock and they're only saying it so they can make even *more* money out of us. You'd be surprised who's taken in by this though. Do you think they 'relax' their dough in the *soukh*? Do you, Pru? In the *soukh*? Maybe next to the carpet shop? Maybe the dough could pull up a little hand-made leather *pouffe* and take some weight off?

Divide the dough into six and search for the rolling pin. Sigh heavily. This is the time for you to add any extra ingredients you may care to dust on. However, it's not going to happen *without that fucking rolling pin*. Stand meaningfully by the drawer where the rolling pin is meant to live. Search for it noisily. Slam the drawer shut. Shout 'It's kicking off, Pru!' and lunge at the nearest customer using whatever utensils are to hand. Or have perhaps been helpfully left to 'soak' by someone.

'it's all
about
emotional
honesty'

THE DANDYLIONS DAMSON PLUM CAKE

This is a charming little pudding that you can run up in next-to-no time — a real lifesaver for those occasions when your partner has got so het up about her blessed choral society singing Die Schopfung (or whatever) that she's not made anything for the poor customers. At this time of year I also think it's a real boon to have something colourful and toothsome to finish off a meal. And by toothsome I mean something so acridly citric and bitter that you'll be practically sucking those bastard teeth out by their little roots. Enjoy!

Takes 15—20 minutes to prepare, 40 minutes in the oven, a further five minutes while you try and find a skewer to 'test' it, can't find one because GUESS WHAT? someone's lost it, so you use the end of a knife, then a further 10 minutes in the oven to over-cook it to deep-golden-to-really-dark brown.

MAKES 15 REALLY MEASLY SLICES

3 eggs
10g caster sugar
250g heavy organic wholemeal flour
1½ tsp baking powder
150g butter (plus a couple of hearty chunks)

3kg whole damsons
  (incl. skins, stones, the lot)
¼ tsp cinnamon
granulated sugar to sprinkle over
  (I wouldn't bother if I were you)

Dissolve the yeast in warm water. Throw the heavy flour into a bowl. Being wholemeal and organic it might well be lumpy. Don't worry about this — it'll be fine. In fact, it improves it.

Make a big well in the flour. Pre-heat the oven 175°C/350°F.

Whisk the eggs and caster sugar with whatever you can find to hand until it's a blob of pale thick ...

You know what? I'm not sure I've got it in me to finish this to be honest — I mean, what is the point? I turn up every morning at about 8.30, meanwhile bloomin' Joan Sutherland here swans in at quarter-past nine or some such, dithers around pom-pom-pomming her ruddy *Schopfung*, while I'm keeping this whole bloody thing afloat. Any problems, who has to sort them out? Who rings the suppliers from Macclesfield when the lentils are lost in transit? Who goes up on the counter to whack the Expelair when it gives up the ghost? Who is prepared to swear at the man in the Cranio-Sacral shop next door when his whale music's too loud? Who has to re-wash all the gritty bits of God-knows-what that come out glued to the tongs because someone doesn't know how to load a dishwasher? Yes, me.

I don't think she's even a vegetarian. I think she only says it because she thinks it makes her sound interesting. Same with the stupid choral thing. Well, that's it. Time to hang up the pinny, shelve the tongs and the Tupperware, and stuff DandyLions. Stuff it stuff it STUFF IT! And sod the lot of you.

Serve warm.

SOMERSET CLING FILM

Honest, Transparent, Unadulterated. Good.

HOME ✷ **ABOUT US** ✷ PRODUCTS ✷ THE TEAM ✷ SHOP ✷ COMMUNITY ✷ CONTACT

What's the story?

We believe that it's always the simple things in life that give the most satisfaction. The simpler the better. Our hand-rolled Somerset Cling Film with its light, transparent, easy-dispensing and 'clingy' film is no exception.

The Williams family of Somerset has been making its own cling film for generations to a special Somerset formula that has been a closely guarded family secret since the 1950s. We guarantee to use only the finest polymers, polyvinyl chlorides and the purest Somerset plasticisers.

The Somerset Promise

NO lumps or bits or anything artificial
NO added sugar, salt or water
NO additives or thickening agents
NO nickel cadmium
NO mercury
Minimal volatile chlorides
NO lactose or gluten
Just yummy home-made fresh cling film

Locally sourced ingredients in our Yeovil blending room

Fritter™

'Wrap' with us!
@somersetclingfilm

SOMERSET CLING FILM
National Country Garden Association
South-West Counties Garden Initiative

This summer, Somerset Cling Film is delighted to be sponsoring the Somerset Cling Film National Country Garden Association South-West Counties Garden Initiative.
The Somerset Cling Film National Country Garden Association South-West Counties Garden Initiative is a drive to encourage gardeners in the South-West counties to cling to the natural heritage of this beautiful part of the world and to take the initiative to open their gardens to the public. As part of its ongoing commitment to natural heritage, Somerset Cling Film is part-funding an award for which all members of the National Country Garden Association who are based in the South-West counties may apply. Successful entries will be judged by a panel of experts and a winner will be announced at the Somerset Cling Film National Country Garden Association Garden Party and Country Fayre by Monty Don on Saturday 16th July.

SOMERSET CLING FILM
Film Festival
(of South-West County Films)

We have recently started our very own Somerset Cling Film Film Festival of South-West Counties Films, a festival that celebrates all that is best about our own local, home-grown cinema. To be included in the Somerset Cling Film Film Festival of South-West Counties Films entries (NB from the South-West *only* please) must be received by 1st September and will be judged by Somerset-related actor and writer **Julian Fellowes** (*Gosford Park, Young Victoria,* please don't mention *Monarch of the Glen*).

PLEASE NOTE
We are now accepting films from Great Britain and Northern Ireland.
AND NOW CROATIA

HERITAGE TRUST

July 1994

ANSTRUTHER LODGE
=================

N O T E S   F O R   V O L U N T E E R S

1. Please replenish promotional stand at start of day.
   Leaflets for Ingleton Caves kept separately in middle
   cupboard. They need folding.Please do so carefully.

2. Childrens' trail colouring sheets need to be photocopied
   regularly. Original is on laminated card in Cash Drawer.

3. Local Geology video is on a loop. (if it gets tangled
   there is a spare in the green cupboard.

4. NO drinks at the till please!

5. Do not give change for pay phone —except in emergencies.

6. First aid kit beneath main kitchen sink. Please warn
    parents about bees in the lavender bushes. They will sting.

7. Diorama flex is frayed and DANGEROUS!!!
   NO unaccompanied children in museum.

8. Watch out for this man. He calls himself an academic.
    SOmetimes accompanied by a film crew.
    DO NOt ADMIT UNDER ANY CIRCUMSTANCES
    *************************** ************

THANK YOU

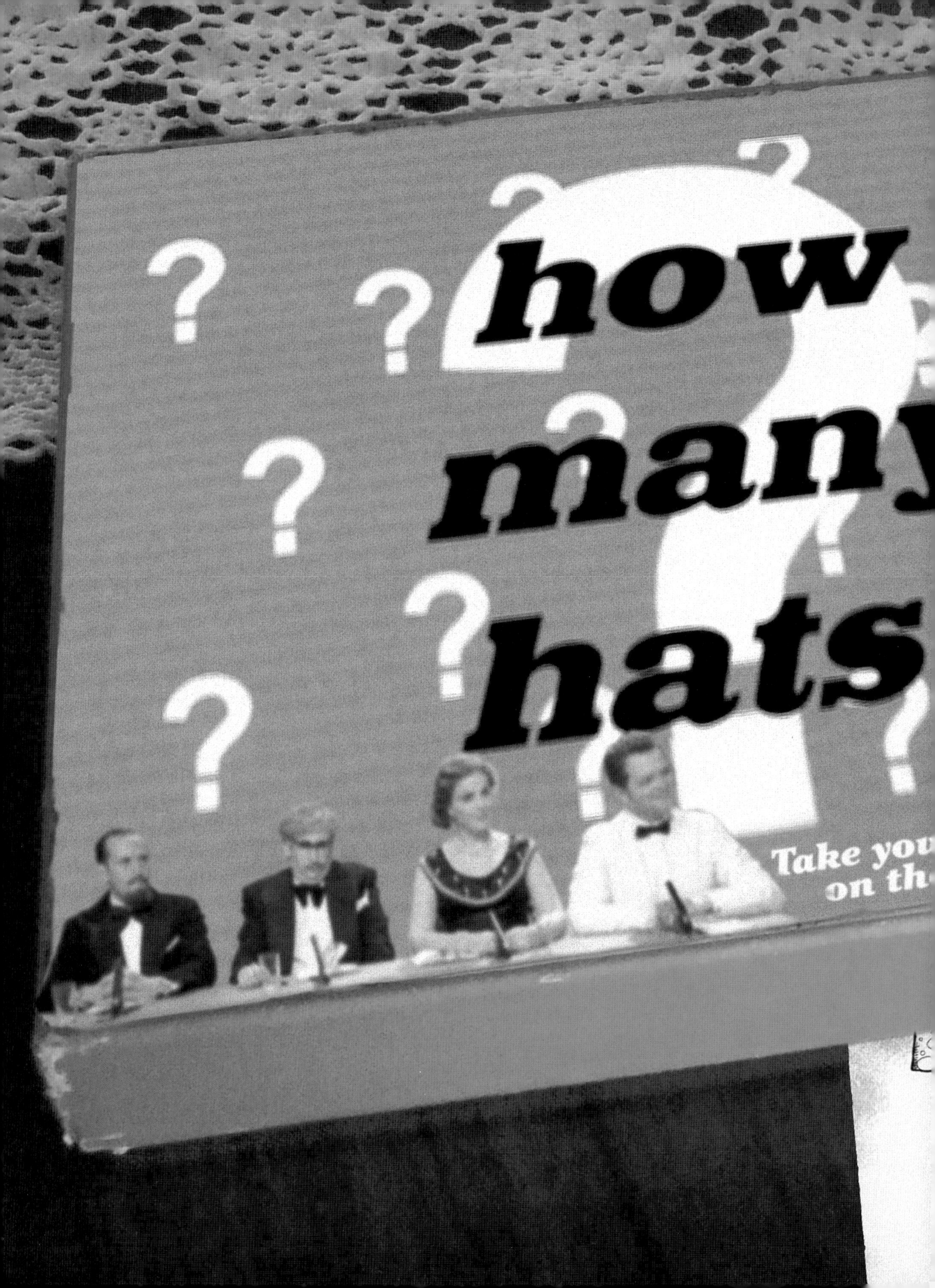
how
many
hats
Take you
on th

Your teatime favourite

- seat
panel

how many hats?

RULES OF PLAY

How Many Hats couldn't be simpler to play. You just need a bit of perspicacity and an enquiring mind.

* First extract the special 'test card' and 'answer card' from the deck. Shuffle the remaining cards thoroughly using your preferred algorithm.

* Proceed to determine the order of play by casting the octagonal dice twice each and ranking the median scores per player. (Naturally, having considered their position carefully, any player may then elect to double.)

* then draw cards in turn. They then study the photograph thereon and in each case try to deduce How How Many Hats? That's right, How Many Hats are they

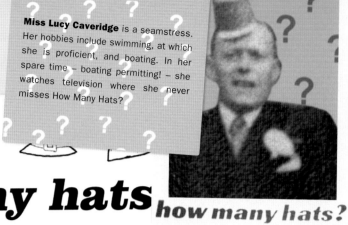

how many hats

RULES OF PLAY

How Many Hats couldn't be simpler to play. You just need a bit of perspicacity and an enquiring mind.

* First extract the special 'test card' and 'answer card' from the deck. Shuffle the remaining cards thoroughly using your preferred algorithm.

* Proceed to determine the order of play by casting the octagonal dice twice each and ranking the median scores per player. (Naturally, having considered their position carefully, any player may then elect to double.)

* Players then draw cards in turn. They then study the photograph thereon and in each case try to deduce How Many Hats the person in the photograph is wearing. How Many Hats? That's right, How Many Hats are they wearing? It may be seven hats or it may be considerably more. Something like twelve hats.

Trial Run. *This 'trial run' is just an opportunity for you to practise before competitive play commences. It will not count towards the final score.*

* Alright, study the photograph on the 'test card' now. As the obverse of the card informs you, this is a photograph of Dr Ranald McPherson. He's a lecturer in Politics at Stirling University. His interests include food, the night sky, and walking with his two sons Duncan and Alasdair.

* How Many Hats is Dr Ranald McPherson wearing? If you need help you may want to consider the following as useful. Is it a prime number? Is the number of hats greater than, or equal to, some other items of clothiture that Dr Ranald McPherson has about him in the photograph? Might the number of hats be divisible by 5, 7 or 11? And if so, to what do the remainders in each case add up? If you were to take the square root of a number, say 64, and subtract the prospective number of hats (provided the prospective number is greater than, or equal to, whichever is the higher of the lowest divisible outcome of the above equation or the sum of the remainders) is the answer lower than the original number divided by 8?

  You are now ready – using the hidden clues we have carefully placed in the picture and the biographical tidbits provided on the back of the card – to state the number of hats you believe Dr Ranald McPherson to be wearing. You will find the answer listed against his name on the special 'answers card'. Don't worry, we've written them upside down so even if you accidentally glance at the card before having done the work, you won't discover the solution. Also we've written the answers in an unspecified old European language which you will have to identify and then research. No one gets something for nothing.

Play Proper. *Having completed the trial run successfully you are entitled to begin 'play proper', as follows:*

* The player who ranked first in the pre-determined order of play shakes a die and takes his turn. Play continues with each player taking a turn successively, one after the other.

* Success at each turn entitles the player to move their counter forward on the play board. The first player to reach the central Hat-Stand will have to answer questions relating to four further cards before nominating a Grand Final How Many Hats card which – if they answer correctly – will see them become the lucky victor.

PRINTED IN THE EMPIRE

how many hats?

Max Storrar is a milk mechanic for one of the largest dairies in the North-West, where he is responsible for the cheese and buttermilk. In his spare time he is a film devotee. He says his favourite film is the rare Vietnamese picture *Thay Phap rau do* (The Red-Bearded Sorcerer) which he has seen twice.

how many hats?

The Revd Thomas Burton is retired but still works occasionally. He is a canon of Southwark Cathedral and sits on the Ely diocesan buildings committee. His hobbies include Ancient Greek and Latin. He has translated many works into modern English including the plays of Aeschylus and Euripides.

ow many hats?

Mrs David Coombes is a mother and housewife. She is married to David Coombes. They have five children: Allan, Berkeley, Shaneeza, Croxley and Cartier. Mrs David Coombes was Watford's gymkhana champion '59 & '61. She has no spare time.

how many hats?

how many hats?

Master Ted Bampton is only 9. Who says boys can't wear multiple hats? Ted attends St Chad's Roman Catholic School for boys in Bury St Edmunds. He has three rabbits and a goldfish and enjoys Gilbert & Sullivan *operas buffas*.

Sacheverell Dave is currently unemployed and unmarried. His hobbies include reading magazines, dating, and applying for job interviews. He enjoys thinking of himself as some kind of inventor. Maybe you'll invent the first Electronic Hat-Counter Mr Dave!

how many hats?

v man

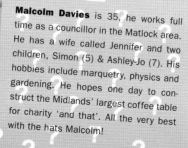

how many hats?

Malcolm Davies is 35, he works full time as a councillor in the Matlock area. He has a wife called Jennifer and two children, Simon (5) & Ashley-Jo (7). His hobbies include marquetry, physics and gardening. He hopes one day to construct the Midlands' largest coffee table for charity 'and that'. All the very best with the hats Malcolm!

ho ma hats? how many ha

Bethany Nation has only recently returned to Battle in Sussex having been abroad for fourteen years working as a missionary in the dark continent. She is capable, trustworthy and has a clean and full driving licence. She has lately lost (or 'misplaced') her faith so 'no more church work please'. She has French and German, and 'bedroom' Spanish. She seems to think this is some kind of labour exchange.

"Lowering the Jolly Roger across the world for 200 years"

http://www.

This website provides general information about Pirates Anonymous – an organisation whose aim is to help men and women give up a life of piracy, looting and all forms of buccaneering.

Thousands of corsairs, filibusters and sea-going marauders have heard or read about the unique fellowship called Pirates Anonymous since its founding in 1795. Of these, hundreds now call themselves members. People who once raided to excess finally acknowledged that they could not handle a smuggler's life on the ocean wave, and now live a new way without it.

The only requirement for membership is a desire to stop pillaging, plundering and rifling. Pirates Anonymous is not allied with Captain Kidd, Calico Jack, the Barbarossa Brothers or any other individual brethren of the coast. Our primary purpose is to stay free of the urge to kidnap, ravage, filch and sack and help other pirates to achieve a life without swashbuckling.

"I used to have many wives and when I tired of one I'd lure her to my treasure room and while she looked at my wealth I'd lock her in and leave her to die. I've given all that up now and settled down in Canterbury where I've started a carpet cleaning business."
"BLACK TOM"

"As a captain of a large sloop I'd think nothing of slitting the nose and ears of a recalcitrant crew member then marooning him on an inhospitable island with only a bottle of spoiled water, a pistol and shot. Since enrolling in an eight-step programme with PA I've given it all up to become a florist." **"RED BEARD aka THE PIRATE KING"**

rates Anonymous

"Lowering the Jolly Roger across the world for 200 years"

Home | **Meeting Finder** | **Links** | **Site map** | **Contact Us**

The Eight Steps

In its simplest form, the PA programme operates when a recovered pirate passes along his story (orally or in the form of a drinking song accompanied by squeezebox) and invites a newcomer aboard. He then shares the heart of the recovery programme as follows:

1. We admitted we were powerless over pirating, that if we carried on we'd be dancing the hempen jig afore too long.

2. We came to believe that we had no choice but to hang up the monkey jacket, abandon the hornswaggle and have nothing more to do with picaroons, cockswains and futtock shrouds.

3. We made a decision to forego the pleasures of the grog, the cackle fruit and the salmagundi.

4. We made a searching and fearless inventory of our crimes, wrongdoings and booty-chests.

5. We admitted to ourselves, and at least one other Jack Tar, the exact nature of our errors.

6. We decided we were entirely ready to forego these defects of character as we removed from our possession all blunderbusses, flintlocks, dirks and cutlasses.

7. We made a list of all the landlubbers we had harmed and asked their forgiveness for braining them with marlinspikes, tying them to the taffrail and shaving their bellies with a rusty razor.

8. Having had a spiritual awakening as the result of these steps, we carry this message to all other brigands and vow never again to fight with lighted matches inserted into our hats and beards.

Registered Office: ✗*, The Isle of Hispaniola, off the Barbary Coast*

"Ask not what your country can do for you . . . ask what you can do for your country."

—President Kennedy in his Inaugural address, Jan. 29, 1961.

Color portrait of President on Page 16.

The Bo

MORNIN

SATURDAY, NO

SHOCK...DISB

John Fitzgerald Kennedy, Born in Brookline, Massachu

Sniper's Bullet Cuts Down
Jacqueline Cra___s Dying
Johnson Sw___McCorm

WA
brought d
Kennedy
immeasur
shocked,

The Bl
Massachuse
Tex., to prin
and in a___

He wr___

The Joy of Sex with Fruit and Vegetables

A Gourmet Guide to Love Making with Nature's Gifts

NEW REVISED ILLUSTRATED EDITION

Jacqueline: 'Oh. No!'

PIPS   *opposite*
Sex play with pips is great because
of their texture – you can handle
them, touch them, insert them and
generally use as one more resource

the watermelon

Ripe, wet, friend of the sailor, the student, lonely males everywhere – the watermelon has been an object of solo amour since at least the Etruscan era. We recommend a trial with an easier-to-manage honeydew or galia before moving to the full delights of the watermelon itself. Which variety is open to discussion: Wax Melon works well, as does Yellow Watermelon. With seeds or *sans* it's very much up to you. Some prefer the feel of seeds – like the hint of a row of teeth; others favour a smoother experience. We go for the former but only because we're too impatient to remove them (and don't like the mess). Other choices include warming the fruit in a low oven prior to use, or soaking in a bowl of steaming water. The size and shape of incision is a matter of some debate. The French favour an oval, the Turks a tighter circular hole. Experiment.

the navel orange

The smaller citrus cousin of the above can provide a remarkably similar experience for the traveller or the spontaneous spirit (not every grocery store will carry melons or indeed other gourds – large oranges can be found anywhere). A word of caution: watch out for any nicks or cuts – the sting of citric acid can be the enemy of even the most priapic.

celery

The uncrowned king of vegetables – present in the tomb of Tutankhamun, referred to in Homer's *Iliad* and notoriously used by Gerda Munsinger, the harlot Soviet Spy, as a means of extracting information from tight-lipped Western agents – celery's erotic uses are bound only by a lover's imagination. Uncut, the generous fronds of its leaves can be used to tickle, caress and generally arouse into a frenzy. Its bulbous and fleshy top-root is often ground into an anaesthetic paste to prolong tumescence. And is there anything to equal the sensation of a crisp petiole (or stalk – to give it its more familiar culinary name) being simultaneously inserted into any number of places. We prefer it as a tool of visual arousal. A plate of celery hearts oiled and dressed can be a surprisingly raunchy sight. Trust us!

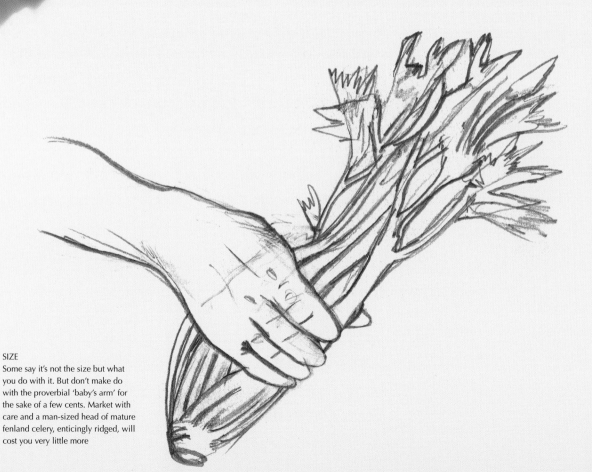

SIZE
Some say it's not the size but what you do with it. But don't make do with the proverbial 'baby's arm' for the sake of a few cents. Market with care and a man-sized head of mature fenland celery, enticingly ridged, will cost you very little more

stone fruits (apricot, peach, nectarine)

Not for nothing is a bottom referred to as a 'real peach'. The cleft and curve of soft fruit has long been celebrated by connoisseurs, and Casanova used to keep a bowl permanently on ice in the summer months. But the great debate – stoned or unstoned – has never truly been resolved. Cutting out the stone is probably the oldest human fruit-related sexual ritual. We're against it. 'To cut out the heart of a peach's secret parts,' said Dr Bulwer 'is against the honesty of nature.' The point is, if you keep the fruit's stone you conserve your options. Women who have experienced both are divided over which is sexier. Some find the stoned centre 'neater' and are often turned off by an unstoned one. Others like the roughness and wholeness of the untampered-with item. Perhaps, like much else, it's a matter of taste. But we prefer to be able to choose our egg with or without salt.

the controversial pickle

Some will balk that we even include this as an entry but our job is to guide – not to judge. We believe the mark of an adult is that he or she is free to choose their own path out of the myriad available. 'But who could dream of doing that to a beautiful cucumber?' asked Catherine the Great upon being shown a pickled gherkin for the first time. A legitimate question and yet there are those who prefer the sharp bouquet of the vinegar-drenched condiment to the smooth aroma of its untrammelled brother. The same goes for the onion – silverskin or shallot – the beetroot and the walnut. Even we would, however, draw the line at the pickled *jalapeño*. Some things are just not meant to be.

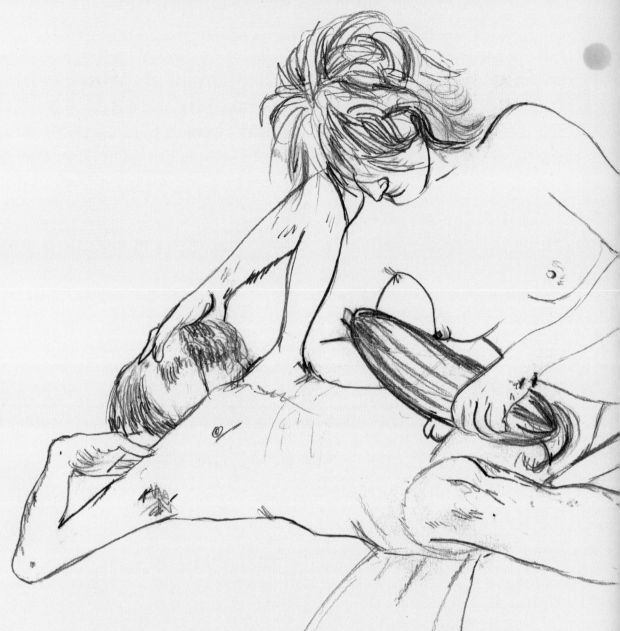

the marrow

Marrow-love has a bit of a chequered history. It's something that most couples try at least once; a few stay with it. The flesh of the *Cucurbita*, to give it its Latin name, is not designed for friction and can rip easily. But many men prefer the sensation of tightness it provides.

The Roman poet Martial threatened to divorce his wife for refusing to indulge him and in the nineteenth century the marrow was seen by the working classes as a form of contraception.

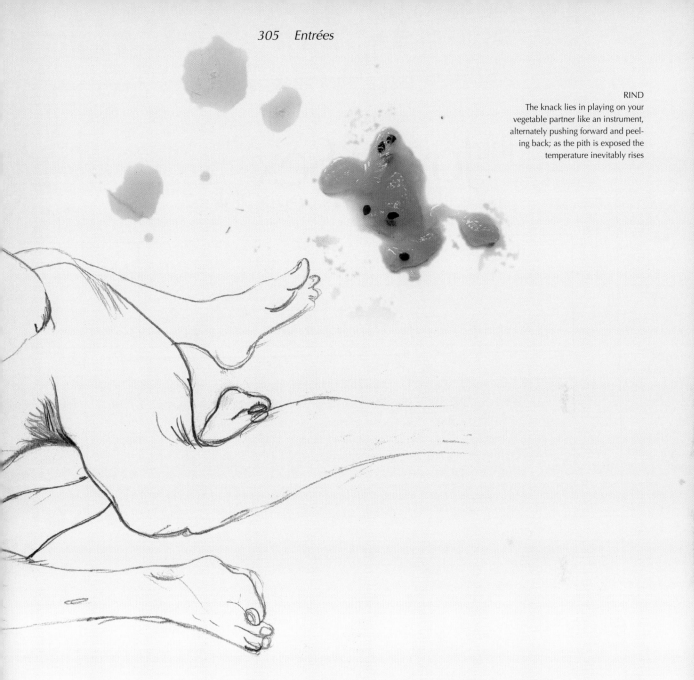

RIND
The knack lies in playing on your
vegetable partner like an instrument,
alternately pushing forward and peel-
ing back; as the pith is exposed the
temperature inevitably rises

Interestingly, though the marrow might be seen as a
phallic object, a very convincing feminine effect can
be created with a bit of carving and shaping. Schopen-
hauer apparently was a bit of a whizz with a craft knife
and could create an anatomically correct pudenda out
of a butternut squash at fifteen minutes' notice.

the piece of
calf's liver

Not strictly a piece of fruit or a vegetable, but keep
an open mind, since a calf's liver can be a remarkable

$9.95

The Joy of Sex
with Fruit and Vegetables

America's Bestselling Gourmet Guide to Love Making with Nature's Gifts. The book that has already shown hundreds of thousands of Americans how to attain the full enjoyment of inventive, carefree sex with garden produce.

"The most joyous and delightfully instructive book on meat-free love and sex published in modern times...." —*Poughkeepsie Sun*

"May be the best thing ever published in its field"

—*Uphill Gardener*

"This must be one of the least inhibited books on sex with fruit ever written"

—*Idaho Review*

"*The Joy of Sex with Fruit and Vegetables* is the Kama Sutra brought deliciously up to date...."

—*Dr. Kirk Lestendall, co-founder of FCUK
(Fruitarian Council of the United Kingdom)*

"*The Joy of Sex with Fruit and Vegetables* is an unusual and outstanding manual that has been edited and written by a gifted professional who really knows his onions. It is far better and saner than any of the 'sensuousness' books of recent vintage...."

—*Ellis Albert, Executive Director,
Institute for Advanced Vegetable Study*

A CORNCOB BOOK
PUBLISHED BY ARMSTRONG AND MILLER
NEW YORK

671-21649-X

ork Times

Weather: Rain, warm today; clear tonight. Sunny, pleasant tomorrow. Temp. range: today 80-66; Sunday 71-66. Temp.-Hum. Index yesterday 69. Complete U.S. report on P. 50.

AY, JULY 21, 1969

10 CENTS

ON MOON
ND ON P
S, PLANT

Cat #1 Net. Wt. / Poids Net. 4.4 Oz. / 125 gr.
Blackberries
Mûres

Berry Lovers!

...tly Healthy

99P

sales@ex...
Distributed...
info@grow... ...h, L.L.C
Exported by... ...C.V
Produce of Mexico / Produit du Mexique
Keep Refrigerated / Laissez au Frigo

A Po...
Is C...

By JOHN NOBLE WILFORD
Special to The New York Times

HOUSTON, Monday, July 21—Men have landed and walked on the moon.

Two Americans, astronauts of Apollo 11, steered their fragile four-legged lunar module safely and smoothly to the historic landing yesterday at 4:17:40 P.M., Eastern daylight time.

Neil A. Armstrong, the 38-year-old civilian commander, radioed to earth and the mission control room here:

"Houston, Tranquility Base here. The Eagle has landed."

The first men to reach the moon—Mr. Armstrong and his co-pilot, Col. Edwin E. Aldrin Jr. of the Air Force—brought their ship to rest on a level, rock-strewn plain near the southwestern shore of the arid Sea of Tranquility.

About six and a half hours later, Mr. Armstrong opened the landing craft's hatch, stepped slowly down the ladder and declared as he planted the first human footprint on the lunar crust:

"That's one small step for man, one giant leap for mankind."

His first step on the moon came at 10:56:20 P.M., as a television camera outside the craft transmitted his every move to an awed and excited audience of hundreds of millions of people on earth.

Tentative Steps Test Soil

Mr. Armstrong's initial steps were tentative tests of the lunar soil's firmness and of his ability to move about

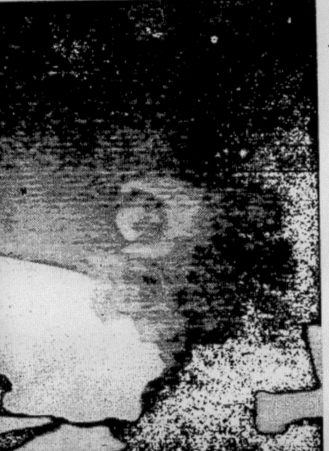

...aft after taking the first step on the surface of the moon

INTERVIEW

VC

John Simmonds

ADDRESS   74Moorside East, Fenham, Newcastle up on TyNe

AGE 29

Education   The Littls Owls Nursery Scohol St Dennys in the Marshsecondry college
Qualifications -- 9 g.s.c.e.s

~~Previsou Experience~~ Missapplication of tiny christs

INTERSETS having ben to the soo called museum of farming, I would never have called myself a farming aficionado. How exactly is cotton organic?
- Denver takes some beating.
- So called experts will shout me down but I have never been to Me. (The trick with the Roulette is double double double every time you lose until you win.) See? Meet *you* in the winne'rs enclosure!

HOBBYS......................Scrabbel and word games of all SORTS!

EMPLOYMNET HISTЄRY

1998-9   Spotty Dogs and Ding-dangs – good for the core
99-01   Chin-ups melon smoothies – yum yum!
01-04   I take a break – went to the Americas cup and traced the San Andreas Faultline from here to Me. Oh I have been to Me - my mistake.

05 till the PRESenT   I run my own company in the city of London--our trading price on the fste 100 index is $72 million ha ha ha.
Not really I have been mooing lawns for friends of my dads.
July'10 Discretion is the better part of valour/

Love weed?

Be a teacher.

www.latestartearlyhome.com

New Brooms

A NEW SPIRIT OF UTILITY IS TAKING FIRM HOLD
in the homes of the style-conscious. But that doesn't
mean that function need trump form or fancy:
designers are upping the ante (and the prices!) of the
most mundane household essentials, tweaking colours and
sneaking luxe materials into unexpected places.

Team these pared-down gems with good English furniture
and a couple of well-chosen antiques, and you'll have this
new look nailed. And – should you need a helping hand –
Use, the hottest new face on the scene, with branches
worldwide, have done the leg work, sourcing and editing
a knockout capsule selection of must-have future classics.

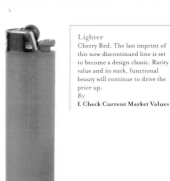

Lighter
Cherry Red. The last imprint of this now discontinued line is set to become a design classic. Rarity value and its stark, functional beauty will continue to drive the price up.
Bic
£. Check Current Market Values

Spork
The clean, succinct lines of this piece from Roberta Kleinworth belie the potency of its message. The subordination of the masculine ForkKnife by the elegant Spoon is reversed in its function when the discomfort of the spoon's handle … oh, it's just perfect. No amount of money is too much to pay for this.
Kleinworth Macheson
£. Too Much

Vase
Vase in recycled glass. Named by its Austrian creator Hans Schlehen 'Vessel of Nothing' when it was first launched at Seattle10.
SchlehenHaus
£. Enough To Buy A House

4th-Century Xin flask stopper
These early Chinese ceramics are ten-a-penny. The market has been flooded with this kind of 4th-century tat for some time, but they're quite decorative and relatively cheap.
Heneage Fass Islamic and Oriental Antiques
£. Enough To Buy You An Island In The Caribbean

Felt tips
A vibrant range of fibre-tip markers in colours devised by Howard Hodgkin RA. Produced in a limited edition on the occasion of the artist's 84th birthday.
Trenemann Heinke
£. Fuck Off

Storage system
Lasercut cartons in a range of sizes. Sculpted cubes manufactured from recycled cardboard and steel staples. Lightweight classics.
Porterhouse & Wedden
£. Right, Fuck Off

Scouring pads
A soaring fanfare of colours in sponge-tops with acrylic bases. A range of designs totalling fifteen pieces. A unique collaborative work from Francis Yquonne and Pål Bremmern.
SPAFF & Co
Try £12,500 for size. OK? That seem alright? Now times it by ten. Then Fuck Off

use where less is more ~~expensive~~

LONDON · MILAN · SWINDON

Book 2 of
THE BELLINGHAM CHRONICLES

"The green tri-suns rose in a perfect line, their distended beams searching the glassy surface of Chewton-St-Mary like the hungry sweep of an old Xerox. The aged warrior stirred from his mournful reverie and contemplated the heavens. By the time those same lights sank behind the molten cliffs of Etteridge, either Lower Dinsbury would have a new emperor or the whole galaxy of Longhoughton would be plunged into a new era of slavery ..."

The Warrior returns! Following the success of *The Moons of Chittleford*, Jeff Benton is back. The Galactical Senate is under dire threat. Matt and Kirsty Durridge, the resurrected leaders of the Vagabonds, run a network of traitors throughout Bickerton that could bring down not only the Upper Citadel but all the departments that together make up the Henderson Centre.

A new emperor is crowned, but is Steve Furlong everything he promises? Jeff Benton is facing the toughest challenge of his life but with the freedom of Haltwell-by-Barrington and the roofing contract of the new Jubilee Hall at stake, nothing is too high a price.

United Kingdom
Australia $2.95 (recommended)

Science Fiction

ISBN 0 14
00.4866 9

Barraclough
DAVE Jr.

The Omega Quadrant of Haltwell-by-Barrington

PART TWO: *Your soaraway Sun serves up a further escalope of extraordinary indiscretions from Mr. Veal—gentleman's gentleman.*

Valet Re-'Veal's All!

∗ ∗ By Our Disgruntled Domestics Correspondent ∗ ∗

There was a certain gentleman of my acquaintance — I won't say employer: that, I fear, would be treading upon the very heels of indiscretion — who was wont to return home in the early hours of the morning with an attendance of some five or six similar rich young men.

Between the hour at which their club in St. James' shut its heavy door and the hour at which it is customary to rise, these men would play upon the benighted capital such acts of devilment that I can hardly mention same without blanching.

Rug

One morning I (sorry, this gentleman's personal gentleman) walked into the study to discover two girls, quite bare, fighting on the hearth-rug.

This in itself was almost a common sight, but on this occasion in order to enliven what had evidently become a contemptibly workaday practice, the young man had removed from the study wall the large stuffed head of a Canadian Caribou and was proceeding to dance around the room with the bare ladies' undergarments hanging from the two score or so points of this cursed creature's antlers.

'What ho,' exclaimed the young prankster on espying a fresh-dressed servant at the door. 'How about getting some liver for these poor girls?'

'Some liver?' enquired the valet.

'And how, pray, would they like their liver? Braised is particularly invigorating, fried no less delicate, and baked nothing but a revelation.'

'No,' cried the young master, lowering the head of the arctic beast for a brief moment, 'Liver for them to fight in! I need it big and raw. The biggest liver you can lay your lily-white hands upon! And some heroin wouldn't go amiss.'

Foie de veau

The poor domestic at this point had no choice but to cycle to Smithfield as fast as the traffic and the rain would allow. There he would doubtless find precisely what the young

Mr. S—. Rumoured to be a member of the influential Idiots Club.

master had ordered. Calf's liver is generally considered to be the best eating, however the gentleman had expressly said that he wished the girls to fight in this specific organ, so he decided to abandon issues of culinary merit and go instead for bloodiness and volume.

Grisly

It so happened that in London the previous night had been a series of grisly murders carried out on the City Road, the corpses from which were being bundled into the Farringdon mortuary at the very moment when our trusty valet was bicycling past. He wouldn't normally have noticed, but his old friend constable Hargreaves was closing up the door of the conveyance as he passed.

They called to one another and the servant pulled up to converse with his old colleague. They talked of this and that and before long the servant had laid out his dilemma before the long arm of the law.

'I'll tell you what,' said Hargreaves. 'I'll very happily fill your panniers with as much bloody gunge as you can manage to

cycle home.'

And so the constable duly filled the servant's saddlebags with the gory viscera of the previous evening's terrible carnage. He was also good enough to spare that fine upstanding man a not inconsiderable quantity of heroin.

All the way back to Mayfair the servant at once chided and congratulated himself on the fortuitousness of his venture.

Coiled

However, on arrival back at the gentleman's home, he discovered that the master and his entourage had decided to go and play golf on Park Lane.

Having no other solution to hand the servant emptied the contents of his panniers into his master's bed. When this was done to his satisfaction he crouched over upon the pristine pillow and coiled down a perfect turd, with the pointed end of which he wrote on the bedroom wall.

'Will that be all, sir?'

EXCLUSIVE
Reader Offer

Pick your way through our 'green and pleasant' land* in style and safety. Are you thinking what we're thinking? Getting a bit like rallying through Helmand down your way? We are delighted to offer our readers the chance to purchase the latest in modern **SatNav** systems, designed and built in the Commonwealth and loaded with all the latest features to keep you on the straight and narrow – at a very special price.

*Also operates in Crown Dependencies and Protectorates

STURDY HOUSING AVAILABLE IN 3 COLOURWAYS:
SMART WHITE (PICTURED), BROWN OR COLOURED

SPECIAL *A&M on SUNDAY* **PRICE**

RRP: £279

£149.95 +P&P
STERLING

Vacuum-cup mounting system fits all popular marques, *including*
Austin Healey ~ Jaguar ~ Riley
Morgan ~ Triumph ~ Wolseley
(NB: also fits all other cars)

Albionic
Steering Clear

'If you haven't already, centrally lock your doors now.
There's an Iceland and an Argos on this street.'

'In 200 yards, on the left-hand side, "faith" school. And I don't
mean a Christian one either. Probably worth driving on
and not looking too closely. Don't know what they're teaching
them in there but it certainly isn't the three Rs.'

'That nice little Turkish man's shop coming up on the left.
Give him a patronising wave and a big smile in 50 yards.'

How many times have you longed for sensible guidance like this through
the badlands that is modern 'broken' Britain? Well, now it's yours, at the touch
of a button, for the special Reader's Price of just £149.95.

BISTROT
ARMSTRONG | MILLER

THE COCKTAILS

A Quick One Round By The Bins
Grey Goose vodka, lime juice, Grenadine syrup
and beaten egg whites

Why Is This Bar Full
Of Eastern European Girls?
Triple Sec, Stolichnaya Strasberi,
José Cuervo Gold and strawberry pulp

The Double Entendre
Kahlua, coconut milk and Baileys Irish Cream
served in a hi-ball

The Unsavoury Friend
Sloe gin, Hendrick's London Gin,
melon and cucumber juice

Persistent Rash
Frangelico, Blue Curaçao, ginger beer,
with a dash of Angostura Bitters

Illegal Mini-Cab
Sambuca, ginger ale, a half of lager
and a packet of dry-roasted peanuts, please

Oh, and just some tap water as well, please

Mid-Coital Soft-On
Finlandia vodka, peach schnapps, pepper grappa,
calvados, absinthe and lime juice

Lazy Eye
Cointreau and Tia Maria dizzied in a tin
over Tango with a pineapple slice

Vodka Suppository
Smirnoff Black vodka, Boots cotton wool

Eamonn Holmes
Tomato consommé, Grey Goose vodka,
Noilly Prat dry vermouth, scotch bonnet chili pepper

The Vermilion Bit
At The End Of Your Penis
Blackcurrant vodka, Grey Goose vodka,
pulped forest fruits, cream

Panorama? On A Sunday?
Champagne, banana purée, Grenadine syrup,
Hennessy XO

Custody Battle
Lagavulin single malt, ginger ale,
egg syrup, brandy sugar

Misspelt Ingredients
Corvoisier, advocat, Triple Seck, King's Gigner

Hasty Sex, Cursory Even
16-year-old saké, melon Tequila, Champagne
with a lime twist

She Strapped One On And Insisted
Plum vodka, apple schnapps, cocaine
and some pink stuff from that bottle at the back without
the label – could be Pepto-Bismol

ALL AVAILABLE IN PITCHERS

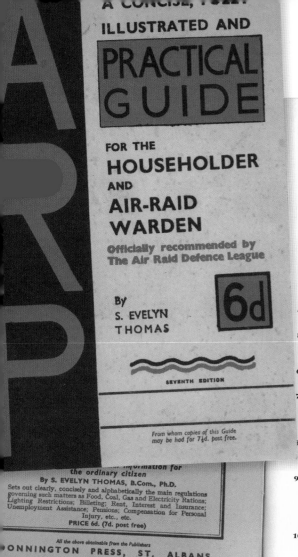

HINTS FOR HOUSEHOLDERS

1. **Keep calm. Don't panic.** Obey instructions calmly and immediately. Especially don't cry because that would be really gay.

2. **If you can get home, do so.** If not, go to the nearest shelter or Refuge Room. If you cannot get to a shelter, stand in a doorway or under an arch, otherwise lie flat on the ground. If you can't lie flat on the ground you is like a major raspberry so make sure you claim, bruv.

3. **Turn off all gas at the meter, put out all fires, and, at night time, darken all the lights visible from outside.** That includes the red one in the window if you is like Mark Henderson from Year 6 and your mum does bed and breakfast for businessmen.

4. **Don't have smoking**, fires, gaslight, plants or flowers in the Refuge Room. Spliff is probably OK though.

5. **Don't wear a gas mask in your Refuge Room** – it is not necessary unless gas is forced in and it will make you look like a remtard.

6. **Don't rush into the street** if you hear an explosion nearby. I mean are you mental or some shit like that?

7. **Don't hang about in the street** if you are forced to leave your Refuge Room, but go immediately to a neighbour's house or to a public shelter. Like I said, are you mental?

8. **Don't interfere with the work of others** such as wardens and fire-fighters. You really is mental blud. Star.

9. **If you do get contaminated with Blister Gas**, throw off your outer clothing, and if you can possibly do so on the spot, wash your body thoroughly in warm soap and water. Be considerate: if you is gyal and raa choong make sure you show everyone your nuggets.

10. **If gas is about and you have to wear your Respirator**, do not remove it without testing for gas. And I don't mean blowoffs, though after three months of powdered egg even Vera Lynn is a danger zone me fam.

... continued from page 190

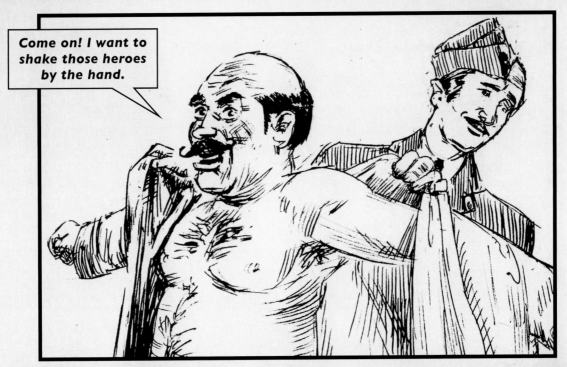

Hitler will send no warning –

because he's a massive remtard

ISSUED BY THE MINISTRY OF HOME SECURITY

Fig. 1: Verrücktespflaster

'pavilion Pavillion (m) *hauptwort*

1. leichtes, üblicherweise offenes Gebäude, das benutzt wird für Unterkunft, Konzerte, Ausstellung *usw.*, *z.B.* in einem Park oder in einer Messe. **2.** getrennte oder verbundene Gebäude, die ein Krankenhaus oder ähnliches bilden. **3.** *in der Architektur:* herausragendes Element einer Fassade, besonders verwendet im Zentrum oder an jedem Ende, und gewöhnlich so verwendet, dass es den Eindruck eines Turms vermittelt.

'paving Pflaster(n) *hauptwort*

1. Gehsteig **2.** Material zum Pflastern **3.** Verlegen eines Gehsteigs.

~ 'block paving Blockpflaster *hauptwort* Pflaster aus Blöcken, *d.h.* festen Steinen, gewöhnlich mit flacher oder ziemlich flacher Oberfläche.

~ 'cobble paving Kopfsteinpflaster *hauptwort* Pflaster das aus Kopfsteinen besteht, *d.h.* Steinbrocken grösser als ein Kieselstein und kleiner als ein Felsbrocken.

~ 'crazy paving Mosaikpflaster *oder* Verrücktespflaster *hauptwort* (¬Fig. 1)

Verrücktespflaster. Du weißt schon. Auf dem Boden. Irrespflaster. Es ist irr. Auf dem Boden. Zerbrochen. Du weißt schon. Die Pflasterstein. Es ist wie eine normale Einfahrt, aber das Pflaster! Ich weiß nicht, wie ich es sagen soll. Es ist einfach Verrücktespflaster. Du weißt, Verrücktespflaster. Der Boden ist verrückt. Statt normalem Pflaster ist es so. Verrücktespflaster. Es ist Verrücktespflaster. Mein Gott! Es ist ganz einfach. Es ist, du weißt schon, normal.

~ *Wie*: ich bin normal, genauso wie mein Frau. Stell dir vor, wir wären Pflaster. Du kannst über uns laufen, es gibt keine Sprünge. Also, wenn wir nicht normal wären, wenn wir nicht normal wären, wären wir verrückt. Ich bin verrückt. Merkst du es? Ich bin zerfallen in allerlei Arten von interessanten Formen.

~ Du weißt jetzt, über was ich rede, nicht wahr? Also los: Verrücktespflaster! Verrücktespflaster! Ich weiss nicht wie ... Verrücktespflaster! Es ist einfach Verrücktespflaster! Verrücktes pflaster! Mein Gott! VERRÜCKTES PFLASTER!

THE SONGS OF DONALD BRABBINS & EDWARD FYFFE

ÉDITIONS A&M
PARIS

I'M A C-NUT!

Words and Music by Donald Brabbins & Edward Fyffe. © Copyright 1958. Reproduced by kind permission. ℗ Dovecote Music Limited.

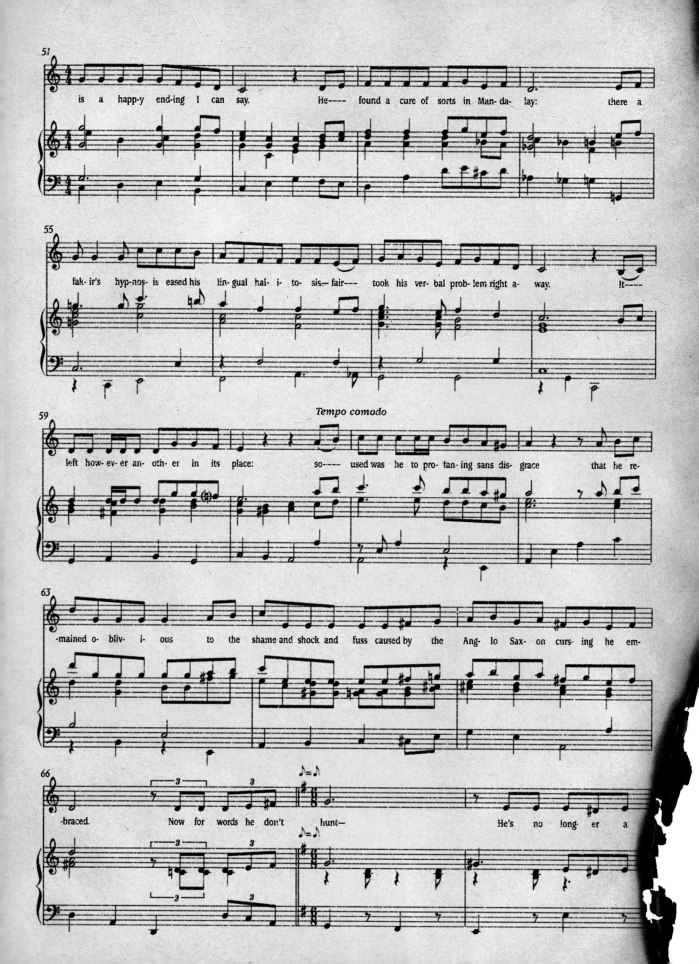

BOOKS of the YEAR

Our seasonal round-up of this year's books, which means we can all stop work in November because this sort of shit fills up pages and pages and can all be done some time over the summer when we're in Tuscany. Mmmmmm.

Donald Brabbins
RECORDING ARTIST

**Screw the Roses,
Send Me the Thorns**
Philip Miller and Molly Devon · *Mystic Rose* ·
277pp · £17.99

This is a beautiful book and one that I shall be gifting extensively around my circle. Devon and Miller (sounds like some ghastly Edwardian cough-drop) reveal the romance 'and sorcery' behind sado-masochism and do so with considerable *élan*.

Much of this will never come off the page in my case, for what I would hope are obvious reasons, but that in no way diminishes the pleasures of the 'ouch' for me. Mrs Brabbins has a mighty strong arm.

Prof. Dennis Lincoln-Park
HISTORIAN

The Dresden Folios
Various · *Dresdener Universitätsverlag* ·
578pp · Priceless

This collection of papers is like a little parable – it was quite possibly the plain inelaborate calfskin of the bindings that preserved the writings within from the fireball that took so much else of this beautiful city.

Found only two years ago, buried beneath the old University Library in Dresden, its very survival and existence is nothing short of miraculous. Even now as I take it in my … oh dear. Er …

Jason Broadreth
BROADCASTER

Grow Your Own Drugs
James Wong · *Collins* · 224pp · £17.99

I saw a poster for this at the station and knew I HAD TO GET THIS BOOK!

What an amazing idea – why's no one done this before It's on all my Christmas lists so hopefully someone will give me it (please please please)!

It looks like if you get it in hardback a) it's a pretty good flat surface for chopping out lines of cocaine, and b) you could make the best roaches EVER out of the dust-jacket. It's like a Swiss Army Knife – it's got everything!!!

Oh. Katy's just told me it's actually about growing medicines and herbal remedies and stuff. Which is still cool.

Baron Anton Von Schleisinger van Hoeken-Hoek von Horschstadt
BON VIVEUR

Paradise
Katie Price · *Century* · 304pp · £14.99

I wonder at the industry of this woman. This is the twelfth of her books that I own and truly she is a phenomenon. Lady Mary Wortley Montagu could not have produced more in her lifetime.

I love the end of the year, when the sun goes down by four and doesn't rise again until eight the following day: a steak 'n' cheese Subway in one hand, a brand new Katie in the other, one very happy *wampyr* in the middle. Bliss.

Rory McCracken
EXTREME CHEF

Great Britain & Ireland 2010
Michelin · *Michelin Guides* · 1080pp · £15.99

This year's book releases have included some truly mouth-watering morsels for the outdoor food-sourcer. Jane Prendergast's *Mushroom A–Z* is one that no wild chef should be without, and Bill Colquhoun's *Splat!*, while not for the squeamish, serves up the best-yet guide to cooking roadkill.

However, both these books are quite dear, especially if you're not sure you'll ever really use them, so you can't go wrong with the good old Mitchy-Lynne. Last one to find a red hotel with all the towers gets the sherry before dinner!

Inès Ligamamada-Teach
PIRATE WIFE

Shell Craft
Annette and Roger Ralle · Search Press Ltd. · 64pp · £5.49

This is a lovely book. *Lovely.* I think of all those *darling* shells from my island back home and I think *I want them.* Ah ha ha ha HA HA ha HA.

Tom doesn't understand the shells, do you, Tom? But for me they are very special. They say we can have *ONE* book and that is very special for us because we only have one other book at home and that is a *book on shells as well*!

We take this shell book Tom, not your smelly pirate book. *THIS.*

Captain Algy 'Algernon' Thompson
RAF PILOT

Captain Flinn and the Pirate Dinosaurs – The Magic Cutlass
Andreae/Ayto · Puffin · 18pp · £6.99

This book is wicked sick yeah? It's about all like dinosaurs and this yeah but they is also pirates? And although it's quite a big book yeah? And long and this, that, and everything else yeah? It's full of like pictures so if you isn't feeling all swotty and doesn't want to like stress out over words and shit you can just like look at the picures, isn't it?

Well nang!

Ken Carpets
ENTREPRENEUR

Ken Carpets Carpet Book
Ken Carpets · Ken Carpets · 18 samples · Free

You get all these Charlies going round saying about all these books that they've read – well, good luck to 'em. But believe you me I you they them, there's only one book I have ever read and there's only one book I *will* ever read.

Come to think of it there's only one book you will ever need to read an' all. The Good Book. I mean you can take all your Counts of Monte Don Corleone Lewis Carroll Ann Duff Hart Davy Jones' Lock-up and shove 'em where the sun don't shine. They'll never give you what Executive Parsley gives you. Never.

Jim Ballantyne
SUPREMO

At Home: A Short History of Private Life
Bill Bryson · Doubleday · 544pp · £20.00

Bill Bryson's book is a collection of facts. *Bingo.* They're presented in strange juxtaposition. *Gotcha.* Bryson's look is very 'Bear'. *Back off, Torquil.*

The book's about his house in Norfolk. *Where in Norfolk?* He doesn't say.

Most books these days are printed on recycled paper. *Received!*

Bill Bryson's an OBE. *Not now Declan, can't you see I'm reading?*

Pru Godwin
VEGETARIAN AND COOK

Grant Me Patience – A Woman's Companion
Various · Virago · 357pp · £14.99

This is a collection of meditations and prayers that has been thoughtfully assembled to answer the needs of the modern working woman. The unique stresses of twenty-first-century womanhood find succour in the empowering writings herein. The rants manage to be spiritual without ramming Christianity down your throat, and many of the moans are viscerally charged and at times quite sharp-edged.

It's a white-knuckle read and never fails to put me on the front foot!

Guy Prentiss
TATTOO ARTIST

Tastes of Byzantium: The Cuisine of a Legendary Empire
Andrew Dalby · I B Tauris · 272pp · £14.99

This is a book that makes me want to shut up the parlour for the summer, climb straight into the soft-top and not stop until I'm amongst the olive groves of the Aegean. Worth every moment of the journey, stopping off to pick up *petits cafés en route*.

Instead I've got to stipple in an osprey on to the hairy arse crack of an extremely flatulent Spaniard. *Merde!*

Paul Pietersen
HOMEMAKER

Blackstone's Statutes on Family Law 2009–10
Mika Oldham · OUP · 672pp · £16.99

Oh it's a nice book this, isn't it? Nice and blue. Not too heavy. Yes, *I know* Sandra, I *am* watching Oliver, he's quite safe – he WANTED to clean the windows.

And how much family law's in here? Wow – masses! I'm just reading a book, Sandra, I am *capable* of doing two things at once, you know.

So does this book tell me everything I need to know about divorce, for example? And custody? Right. Oh my *God*, Oliver. My *baby* – are you alright? Talk to me! SAY SOMETHING! Oliver …

Yup, I'll be reading this cover to cover.

Terry Devlin
ROYAL EXPERT

Royal Sex: Mistresses and Lovers of the British Royal Family
Roger Powell · Amberley · 336pp · £20

This is a book that promises more than it could ever deliver. The 'British Royal Family', it says on the cover – hoping that we might think beans were going to be spilt about Her Majesty The Queen, her royal consort His Royal Highness the Duke of Edinburgh, His Royal Highness the Earl of Wessex, The Duke of Gloucester, his Royal Highness Prince Michael of Kent, Sandringham, Birkhall, the Queen Mother's Private Retreat near Balmoral, Lady Sarah Chatto – formerly Armstrong-Jones – and many many more.

But they're not.

High Prince Alto Pharius the Dread
SYBARITE

Mlinaric on Decorating
Mirabel Cecil and David Mlinaric · Francis Lincoln · 224pp · £35

This book makes me homesick – I turn the pages and feel the years fall away. Beauty like this is so rare in this wretched era, so rare.

I haven't truly 'eaten' since Horschstadt took me to a T'Pau concert in 1987 and even that was a girl so ripped on amphetamines that I was seeing little pink daisies everywhere I looked for weeks. I think that was the drugs.

Roger Graham
ACCOUNTANT

A Dance to the Music of Time (all four movements)
Anthony Powell · Chicago University Press · 2978pp · £199.99

Holly has given me this delightful collection of classic Powell, which I am ashamed to admit I have never read. But now we are going on holiday and, armed with my iPod, my noise-cancelling headphones – another generous present from Holly – and nearly 3,000 pages of wonderful prose, I shall be in a world of my own – seventh heaven!

Yvonne Hammond
RETAILER

Sumo
Helmut Newton · Taschen GmbH · 480pp · £99

I was sent this by one of our interior people to 'give me some ideas'.

Well, it gave me the idea that somehow I wouldn't be getting my pubic department out for the cameras any time soon. Some of the wotsits I saw in here put me in mind of when our spaniel had his operation. That fur didn't grow back for months. If you ever got me posing like that everyone would be wondering when Dennis the Menace would be coming to get his dog back.

BOOK LAUNCH
(draft 14.7, B&X RW orig. JD)

INT. A BOOK LAUNCH IS IN PROGRESS. RANDOM
CELEBRITIES AND PUBLISHING TYPES DRINK WARM WINE
AND MAKE STILTED CONVERSATION.

XANDER:
Sorry everyone ... Dermot? Shami? If we could just have a bit
of schtum?

// THE ROOM FALLS SILENT. EVERYONE LISTENS WITH RAPT
ATTENTION.

XANDER:
I just wanted to say a few words, if I may, on this, the launch of
our very first Armstrong and Miller comedy book ...

// BEN AND XANDER SHARE A FOND LOOK. ARE THEY GAY?
IT'S AMBIGUOUS.

XANDER:
And I think you'll all agree she's looking mighty fine.

// HOLDS UP COPY OF THE BOOK.
If anyone is wondering, the silver lettering on white thing was
my idea.

// MOMENT OF SELF-AWARENESS.
It's not important.

BEN:

// SOTTO, TO DERMOT MURNAGHAN.
He's got one of those white iPhones, like girls have? Ripped it
off from that ...

XANDER:
The point is, we owe a huge debt of thanks to so many people
here for making this something that we are truly proud of.

// THIS APPEARS SINCERE AND PEOPLE ARE UNCERTAIN
HOW TO REACT. IS THERE GOING TO BE A JOKE?

XANDER:
Firstly we'd like to thank Tim and Jeremy. Tim for his
outrageously brilliant design, dedicated hard work and tireless
originality; and Jeremy, as ever, for his untempered passion
and gifted co-writing.

// CLEARLY THERE ISN'T. SOME COUGHING AND ROLLING OF
EYES AS EVERYONE SETTLES IN FOR THE LONG HAUL.

XANDER:
Then of course there's our truly inspirational editor, Antonia ...
where's Antonia?

// KATIE DERHAM MAKES THAT DRUNK SIGN WHERE YOU TIP
BACK AN IMAGINARY GLASS, AND THAT SLASH-ACROSS-
THE-THROAT SIGN TO MEAN 'GONE HOME'.

XANDER:

Again? Ooh dear. So ... Well, also huge thanks to Max who drew the comic strip ... thank you so much for that – it's everything we hoped it might be.

MAX STARES BACK IMPASSIVELY. JAMES MAY LOOKS AT HIS WATCH.

XANDER:

Saskia at Toff, who got our shit together; Josephine, our peerless PA; Luigi, our silver-tongued agent; Hannah, our desk editor, Maddie, the legal eagle and everyone at our publishers Little, Brown ... Caroline, Dom and Ben and everyone who works on the TV show and put so much into the look and feel of these characters ... anyone else?

BEN:

The writers?

XANDER:

God yes, what am I doing? And all our fabulous writers who created the characters in the first place – Simon Blackwell, David and Ali, David and Nico, Ali Griggs, Andy and Kevin, Bert and George, Graham Linehan, Jamie and Louis, Joel and Jason, Mark and Justin, Richard and Anil and others ... Without you we'd be nothing. You really are the absolute cream of the crop, and we can't believe how lucky we are to work with you. Thank you.

A TURNING POINT. EVEN THE MOST CYNICAL HACKS IN THE ROOM ARE MOISTENED BY THIS HEARTFELT TRIBUTE.

XANDER:

Anyway, we've laid on a little treat for you all in the next room; so please, enjoy. You really have earned it. Here's to 'The Armstrong & Miller Book'!

EVERYONE: (IMMEDIATELY, RAISING GLASSES)
The Armstrong & Miller Book!

COMMUNICATING DOORS OPEN REVEALING A SUMPTUOUS BUFFET AND DANCE FLOOR. HOLLY WILLOUGHBY BEGINS TWIRLING TO THE SCISSOR SISTERS.

BEN AND XANDER WAIT UNTIL EVERYONE LEAVES. THEN XANDER LEANS FORWARD AND SPEAKS INTO A HITHERTO UNSEEN MICROPHONE.

XANDER:

Kill them.

346